Bench Notes II

A Judge's Continued Reflections and Advice for His Grandchildren

Judge Paul A. Chernoff

Dedicated to:
My loving wife Lynn and wonderful son Steven who lived through
these vignettes over the decades and helped recall them, and my
dear daughter-in-law Naina who has encouraged this work for
their children
Rayan, Dhillon, and Aliya.

My close friends, seen in several vignettes, Judge John C. Cratsley,
Judge Edward M. Ginsburg, Dr. Robert L. Lebowitz,
Mr. C. William Mathisson, and
the late Judge Robert H. Bohn.

My editor and friend, Dee Netzel.

A special thanks to Robert Lebowitz, Norma Horwitch, and
Lynn Chernoff
who commented early and often on the contents.

Bench Notes II, A Judge's Continued Reflections and Advice for His
Grandchildren

Copyright © 2014 TXu001934326 by Judge Paul A. Chernoff

ISBN: 978-1-4951-3173-8

Printed in the United States of America.

Cover design by Jonathan Cahill.
Front cover photo by Alex Jones.

Dear Rayan, Dhillon, and Aliya,

I was going to name this second book *Primum Non Nocere*, which is the oath taken by physicians. It translates as, "Above all, do no harm." Of course, we all, including doctors, do at least some harm to others in the course of a day. However, it is important to live one's life being aware of what harm or injury we are causing because we should attempt to minimize that harm and help people who have been harmed by us or by others. Although I am again presenting my experiences and thoughts with the format of vignettes, you will see that here I often point out the moral to the particular story. I chose the title of *Bench Notes II, A Judge's Continued Reflections and Advice for His Grandchildren* to give some continuity between the two books.

      As we age, our memory of things that happened long ago seems to improve. What I find just as remarkable are the things that jog these memories. For example, being passed on the highway by a speeding car or glancing at an inscription on a building. It is a treat to tell you these stories in person, but I want you to have something to jog your memory in future years.

Love you always,

Grandpa

VIGNETTES

Commitment

My mother, Thelma "Tommy" Chernoff, used to brag that between her, her two sisters Evelyn Croog and Sonya Gurian, and her brother Lester Aaronson, they had accrued almost 250 years of marriage. Grandma and I celebrated our 50th wedding anniversary this year and, together with my brother Bob and sister-in-law Judy, we have almost 110 years of marriage. Great-Granddad Art and his wife Evelyn also celebrated almost 65 years of marriage. These 425 years represent a serious resolve and commitment that we have made to one another. I introduced my best friend Harvey to my cousin Naomi and now they have been married for 52 years.

Each of our relationships has undergone difficult times due to stressful life situations that have grated on emotions and nerves. For Grandma and me, it was difficult as a young married couple to deal with our situation involving our brain-damaged autistic child, your Uncle David. This was at a time when the norm was to hide disabilities from the public view and to not even discuss the well-being of the person with close family members. Our commitment to one another survived this. The marriage bonds of the other married couples in our family have also been tested over the years.

I have performed more than 100 weddings and I know of only 6 divorces from that group to date. That success record far exceeds the national average of about a 50% success rate. Obviously, some marriages are a mistake from the very beginning, while others dissolve because of unforeseen situations or reasons of physical or mental health. Unfortunately, I see relationships in court that lack real commitment and simply fall apart for the convenience of the parties who feel they need a change of scenery. One reason that I love the "Until Death Do Us Part Probationer" vignette (page 44) is that it involves a couple whose marriage fell apart for many reasons. As older and wiser individuals, they made a new commitment to remarry at a time when the woman was nearly recovered from a serious medical condition and the man was making excellent strides in addressing a problem with pills.

Nothing can be more challenging than keeping a commitment to another through the decades. Yet, nothing can be more rewarding.

A Pearl from Our Poet Laureate

My grandfather, S. D. Aaronson, taught me to memorize poetry at age five, and I am still doing it 70 years later.

In the summer of 2001, Grandma and I were reading in bed at the farmhouse in Vermont. I was learning Robert Frost's "Once by the Pacific," a poem that describes a terrifying ocean storm as seen from the shore. Grandma and I agreed that Frost must have been writing about the Japanese sneak attack on our naval base at Pearl Harbor in Hawaii that resulted in the U.S. declaring war against Japan during World War II. President Roosevelt described the date of the attack, December 7, 1941, as a "Date that will live in infamy."

After the terrorist attacks on the World Trade Center in New York and the Pentagon in Washington, D.C., on September 11, 2001, we Americans saw that date as one that would also live in infamy. A couple of months later, I attended a talk given by America's Poet Laureate, Robert Pinsky, at Middlesex Community College in Lowell. A member of the audience asked Dr. Pinsky how long after a tragedy it is before there are meaningful literary works on the subject. To everyone's surprise, Poet Laureate Pinsky said that the most significant writing about a tragic event normally occurs about fifteen to twenty years before the event.

I came home and told this to Grandma and we immediately researched the writing of "Once by the Pacific." Sure enough, it was written in 1928, almost 15 years before the attack on Pearl Harbor.

I believe that our Poet Laureate was telling us that these searing events delay quality creative writing about the significance of those happenings, but we can look to the past, whether it's 50 years to Robert Frost or 400 years to William Shakespeare, for universal truths and prophetic writings to give meaning to the present.

"Once by the Pacific"

The shattered water made a misty din.
Great waves looked over others coming in,
And thought of doing something to the shore
That water never did to land before.
The clouds were low and hairy in the skies,
Like locks blown forward in the gleam of eyes.
You could not tell, and yet it looked as if
The shore was lucky in being backed by cliff,
The cliff in being backed by continent;
It looked as if a night of dark intent
Was coming, and not only a night, an age.
Someone had better be prepared for rage.
There would be more than ocean-water broken
Before God's last Put out the Light was spoken.

Grandpa Missed the Boat

How many people do you know who inadvertently missed a private meeting with the President of the United States? Well, I did.

Captain Arthur L. Wardwell, your great-granddad, supervised the building of the ship USC&GS *Oceanographer* in Jacksonville, Florida, and he became its first captain. Before taking the ship around the world, Capt. Wardwell sailed it to the Navy Yard in Washington, D.C., where it was formally commissioned by President Lyndon B. Johnson. Grandma and I were living in Washington, D.C., at the time. I was attending George Washington University Law School and Grandma was translating Russian at the Library of Congress.

We were invited guests to the commissioning ceremony on July 13, 1966. Grandma, Great-Grandma Evelyn, and I were to board the ship to meet with President Johnson. I stayed behind for a couple of minutes to take photos of them from down below on the dock. When I tried to board the ship, I was told that no one else could board for security reasons. On board, your grandma and your great-grandparents met the President and chatted with him.

Well, I had a nice view of the ceremony where both President Johnson and Great-Granddad were featured speakers.

If I learned one thing from this experience, it is that one should always pay attention, ask questions, and plan accordingly.

Lady Bird Johnson,
Great-Granddad and
President Johnson at the
ship's commissioning
(NOAA USC&GS Central Library)

Princess Grace and Great-Granddad on
board the *Oceanographer* in Monaco
(NOAA USC&GS Photo Central Library)

Anchors Aweigh

There were four officers on the ship *Bowie*. Bill Mathisson was the second officer and I was the third. We spent April through October surveying waters in Cook Inlet, the lengthy waterway (150 miles) from the Gulf of Alaska to Anchorage. That far north the tidal range is over thirty feet and the current is fierce in the inlet, which has a sandy bottom. We anchored the ship one night and, to our dismay, the combination of tide, current, and sandy bottom caused us to drag anchor and the ship went aground. It listed so far that we thought we might be in danger of capsizing. Fortunately, the tide reversed and righted the ship. In the naval services, going aground places a serious blemish on the record of the ship's captain, who may never receive another command. I don't believe our captain was disciplined. One of the ship's two propellers bent when the ship hit bottom and there may have also been some damage to a rudder.

After we returned to Seattle for the winter, the ship was placed in dry dock for maintenance and repairs. The propeller was replaced and the rudder fixed. My father, William Chernoff, felt I must have been at least partly responsible for the destruction of U.S. property and that the government was going to send him a bill. I think it took several years before he was convinced that he was off the hook. My mother, Thelma (Tommy) Chernoff, and I thought it was humorous, but now, decades later, I'm charmed that he felt this responsibility for me.

USC&GS *Bowie*

Was It All for Naught, I Think Not

Have you ever sent a lengthy e-mail to someone only to find that it disappeared into cyberspace? Or, better yet, have you spent significant time composing something on paper or on your word processer and then learned that it was inadvertently destroyed or deleted? If so, then you must have been very frustrated and felt that all your work was for naught.

Grandma and I celebrated our 50th wedding anniversary this year with a trip on the Alaska Ferry with Bill and Margaret Mathisson. In 1963, Bill and I were junior officers on the ship *Bowie*. We followed the Alaska Ferry route from Seattle to Anchorage and spent more than four months surveying and charting the ocean floor and coastline from the Gulf of Alaska for one hundred-fifty miles to Anchorage. We, and our shipmates, spent all day, every day collecting precise survey data for the publication of accurate nautical charts. About six months after we completed our work, the so-called "Good Friday Earthquake" occurred. It caused a great deal of damage to property, completely changed the contour of the ocean bottom, and moved masses of land horizontally and vertically. There were 139 people killed. In some areas the land rose 30 feet and in others it sank 8 feet. After spending thousands of hours on our survey work, no part of it was accurate after the earthquake and we thought that our season's work was for naught. However, I was later to learn that there were surveys of the same area soon after the earthquake and that geologists benefitted greatly from comparing our survey data with that of the new survey. Our work helped them quantify how much the ocean's bottom was impacted and how and where the land mass moved. So, our work was not for naught, it simply taught a different, but important lesson.

Back to your composition. After the first one was inadvertently destroyed, chances are that you re-wrote the composition and it was far better than the first one. Unbeknownst to you, your mind was working on it between the two writings. See, it wasn't for naught.

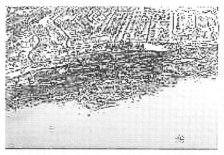

(Photo courtesy of University of Washington)
Good Friday Earthquake, March 27, 1964

A Hallmark Event

Grandma sent a birthday card to Julie Ginsburg that, at first glance, was very funny, and, on reflection, was very insightful. It read: "No woman has ever shot a man while he was doing the dishes."

A person, good or bad, is likely to be reluctant to hurt or slight someone who is doing something good for another. A colleague of mine works in a public defenders' office. He was confronted on the street by a robber with a gun. My colleague had the presence of mind to say that he represented poor people and that the robber probably knew some of his clients. The robber put the gun in his pocket and walked away. A similar example concerns a woman in the Boston area who was confronted by an assailant. The elderly woman said to him, "Don't I know your mother? She's really a nice lady." The assailant fled.

When I was a junior officer, driving from Boston to Norfolk to board my first ship, I drove in the wrong lane around Dupont Circle in Washington, D.C. A police officer stopped me and said that I had committed nine motor vehicle infractions. When he learned that I was on my way to my ship at the Norfolk Naval Operations Base, he wished me luck and let me go with a verbal warning.

There is hardly a downside to doing the right thing.

Dupont Circle, Washington, D.C.
(U.S. Geological Survey)

History or Horror

I was the assistant navigation officer on the ship *Pathfinder* in 1962 when we sailed from Pearl Harbor in Hawaii to Christmas Island, about 1,000 miles south and near the equator. We were participating in a U.S. Navy operation where our task was to map an area for observation ships to monitor the last above-ground hydrogen bomb test explosion. After finishing our work, we sailed back to Hawaii. When we were more than 100 miles north of Christmas Island, it looked like we could see a mushroom cloud, but we were not certain.

Months later, the officers on our ship received certificates from the Navy with a large mushroom cloud icon. The text on mine read that the U.S. Navy thanked Lieutenant Junior Grade Paul A. Chernoff for participating in this important nuclear project.

I kept the certificate for at least twenty years and, given my strong aversion to nuclear weapons, one day I simply destroyed it. It didn't take me long to regret doing so because I have denied you, my grandchildren, a piece of history. There is a common expression, "Look before you leap." In this instance I failed to look into the future before leaping and I destroyed something I should not have.

Learning

Traditionally, we learn from teachers with professional credentials. However, it would be a mistake to conclude that our education ends there. We would miss a lot if we did not avail ourselves of less formal sources. When selecting a foreperson of a jury, I almost always appoint a person who has children because our children provide us with an additional education.

When I was a junior officer at sea, I spent many hours with non-officer crewmembers. Although many of these sailors did not finish high school, most had amassed an incredible amount of knowledge over their own careers. In the evening I would join a group of them on the stern of the ship *Bowie* where they taught me how to tie nautical knots. To this day, I can tie a reverse bowline with my eyes closed. From them, I also learned about signs of change in the weather, engine repair, and life itself. I shared with them what little can be learned from a 22-year-old.

In retrospect, there were at least three benefits to be gained: I learned many important things from them; they learned a few things from me; and, perhaps most importantly, they learned that I respected them and, for that, they gave me their loyalty during my entire tenure on the ship. I felt when they called me "Sir," it was not just because of the bars on the uniform.

Those lessons at sea have stood me well throughout my career. I accompanied parole officers when they were making home visits to parolees. Once again, I learned much from them, they learned some things from me, and I enjoyed their trust throughout my years as Chairman of the Parole Board. The same has been true in each and every courthouse where I have worked over the past 35 years.

In a sense, I think that I owe these lessons in life to Seaman Eddie Starrico, who taught me my first nautical knot.

Bowline Knot (Grog, Animated Knots)

My Consciousness of Guilt

Recently, while driving on the Massachusetts Turnpike (Mass Pike) from the courthouse in Springfield to my home in Newton, a car passed me at a very high speed and that jogged my memory from some forty years ago.

Governor Francis Sargent appointed me to the position of Parole Board Chairman. His Lieutenant Governor was Donald Dwight, who came from Holyoke in western Massachusetts. Dwight spent weekends at home and returned to Boston each Sunday afternoon. One Sunday, he was passed on the Mass Pike by an official state vehicle traveling at an excessive speed and he noted the number on the license plate. Monday morning, his administrative assistant called me and said that Dwight had observed a Parole Board vehicle traveling at an unsafe speed and that the parole vehicles were under my authority. With trepidation, I proceeded into the lower garage of the state office building in search of the vehicle in question. I thought about how I could find out who was driving the vehicle, how I could explain my lack of knowledge, and how I could prevent such a happening in the future. In other words, I felt so guilty that I had already convicted myself.

When I found the vehicle with that license plate, I saw that it, and the license plate, had months of dust covering all surfaces. On further investigation, I learned that the vehicle had not been on the road for over one year, that it had no battery, and the starter was inoperative. The cloud of guilt lifted as I reported my findings and offered to take pictures for the Lt. Governor. I was told that my word was good enough and that he must have made a mistake recording the license plate.

I have often given the following instruction to a jury in a criminal case: *"Please also bear in mind that a person having feelings of guilt is not necessarily guilty in fact, for such feelings are sometimes found in innocent people."*[1]

---

[1] § 4.19 of *MCLE Massachusetts Criminal Practice Superior Court Jury Instructions*. From the standard instruction on "Consciousness of Guilt" when there is some evidence in the case that the person charged might have left the scene, concealed himself, or given inconsistent versions to the authorities.

Try to Do No Harm

There are always risks of rehabilitation. I was Chairman of the Parole Board that paroled a person who subsequently committed a murder. Also, we paroled a man who later sued me over the procedures used to send him back to prison after he committed a new crime. However, I also took many risks that worked out well.

I received a telephone call from a man in California who told me he had been released on parole from a Massachusetts prison ten years earlier after serving two years on a burglary case. While on parole, he left without permission and settled in California. I learned that he was an accomplished sculptor and that he and his wife owned a sculpture studio in Sausalito, across the Golden Gate Bridge from San Francisco. He said that he could no longer live as a fugitive and wanted to come back and serve the three years left on his sentence. He said that he had been a model citizen since he arrived in California and that he was known in his community as a gifted artist.

By coincidence, I was going to a meeting in San Francisco the next month. I told him that he could meet me in the lobby of my hotel where I would conduct a parole violation hearing. The California parole authorities conducted an investigation at my request and confirmed that the man had been a model citizen. He and his wife appeared in the hotel lobby and we had a very pleasant meeting. He told me that he heard that in California a return to prison would be automatic for this kind of violation and he was prepared to surrender himself in Massachusetts. I told him to go back to work and that I would make a report to the Massachusetts Parole Board.

My colleagues and I on the Massachusetts Parole Board agreed that returning him to prison would serve little purpose. The man continued to do well and did not violate our trust. I am proud that we elected "to do no harm."

Human Frailty

Recently, when leaving the Hall of Justice Courthouse in Springfield for a luncheon meeting, I looked up and immediately knew this story had to be told.

When I was chairman of the Massachusetts Parole Board, I hired new parole officers who by law came from the ranks of prison guards and social workers. I learned very quickly that former prison guards usually made better parole officers than former social workers. This surprised me because the social workers were better educated, having college degrees in the behavioral sciences.

The former prison guards did not hold the parolees they supervised to a standard of perfection. They understood human frailty and that a person with a troubled past, who was trying to succeed on parole, might well have an occasional lapse that did not warrant a return to prison. The former social workers tended to see a parolee's setback as a treatment failure that presumptively required re-incarceration.

Back to the Hall of Justice with its inscription quoting Sir Thomas Noon Talfourd, an English jurist: "Fill the seats of justice with good men—not so absolute in goodness as to forget what is human frailty."

Eddy at Midnight

One summer when your dad was a teenager, we hosted Frederic Chabrand, the son of a Justice of the Supreme Court of France. He was about a year older than your dad and far more daring, especially when it came to scary Vermont cemeteries at midnight.

One passes the Eddy house when driving to our farm in Chittenden. It is now owned by a New Jersey ski club. One hundred years ago it was owned and occupied by the Eddy family, who were said to be able to communicate with the spirits of people who had died. They held séances at the Eddy House that were attended by many, including your great-great-great-grandfather. Candlelight processions sometimes led people deep in the woods to Honto's Cave, the burial site of a Native American member of the group. The enormous glacial stone there carries markings that some think were carved by the Vikings. This theory has been rejected by investigators. William Eddy conducted séances throughout the area, including New York State. He was considered the leading medium of his time.

William Eddy is buried in the Eddy Plot, at a dark edge of the Horton Cemetery on a hill just outside the village of Chittenden. There are dead trees with overhanging branches that make creaking noises and cast eerie shadows. There are also a few shiny trinkets that have been placed on the headstone.

We have always found the Eddy Plot to be scary, even on the brightest of summer days and we used to dare your dad when he was a teenager to go alone to the Eddy Plot at night—especially at midnight—and he always declined.

Frederic, our French daredevil, convinced your dad to go to the Eddy Plot at midnight. I drove them to the cemetery gate at 11:55 P.M. and they walked up the path into the cemetery. I could see from my car that their flashlight was traveling very slowly towards the rear of the cemetery. After a minute or two, I saw the flashlight's beam flying toward the exit with the boys running. They jumped into the car and we sped away. They excitedly explained they saw and heard something unexpected. I will leave it to you to find out from your dad what it was and then tell me.

The Path to Horton Cemetery

"William H. Eddy
Passed to Spirit Life
Oct 25, 1932 Aged 99 Yrs. 4 mos."

When I think of your dad and the Eddy Plot, I also think of the last stanza in "Desert Places" by Robert Frost:

They cannot scare me with their empty spaces
Between stars—on stars where no human race is.
I have it in me so much nearer home
To scare myself with my own desert places.

Incivility

An attorney telephoned asking that I call him about a parole client. I did not return the call because I knew he wanted to talk about a case with little merit. Weeks later, I saw the attorney at a meeting and he expressed disappointment in me. He said that even if his client was not worthy of a favorable decision, he was a professional who deserved to have his call returned. He was absolutely right and I never forgot that lesson in basic civility. Since then, I attempt to return all calls, letters, and e-mails. The attorney's disappointment in me has made me particularly sensitive to people who do not return my calls or answer my letters or e-mails.

Last summer we purchased a kitchen range for the farmhouse in Vermont from a large appliance company. The range arrived damaged and the delivery person left with it. It took me eight months to receive my money back. I called the company fifteen times over eight months and each time someone promised to call me back and never did. I became angry and determined to get results. Finally, I wrote a letter to the company's president, which resulted in an appropriate response.

New large windows were installed at the farmhouse. Unfortunately, they fogged up each morning to the surprise of our contractor. I called the window manufacturer each week for ten weeks and the recipient of each call promised me that someone knowledgeable from the company would return my call. No one did. Finally a local company representative inspected the windows as a favor to our contractor.

I am afraid that science and technology are conspiring to promote incivility. The advent of "call waiting" and other such devices enable people to shun others without them knowing it. Unreturned calls and unanswered e-mails or letters do drive me a little crazy. I hope you feel likewise.

Just Say No

In 1982, we were visiting Uncle Bob on the New Jersey Shore when I received a call to meet with Governor Edward J. King. We cut short our vacation and returned to Massachusetts. I had never met Governor King and our conversation started with small talk about jogging, which we had in common. Then he said that he wanted to consider me as the next Commissioner of Correction based on my performance as head of the Parole Department for four years and my service on the bench for six years. I knew that the Department of Correction had seen its share of recent trouble with inmate riots and confrontations with the guards and their unions.

My first response to Governor King was that I would not want to embarrass him. He was an outspoken advocate for the death penalty and I was staunchly opposed to it. I said that I would not permit an execution if I were commissioner. The Governor's legal counsel said this was not an issue because it took ten years between conviction and the carrying out of a death sentence. We then spoke of the challenges facing the commissioner and how they might be addressed. At the conclusion of the meeting, Governor King said that he wanted to appoint me, but he needed a couple of days. I said that I too needed a few days. He assured me that if I accepted the position and later wanted to return to the bench it would be no problem.

I talked to many people over the next few days and most encouraged me to accept the position. I had administered the Parole Board with about 125 employees and an amicable union. The Department of Correction had thousands of employees with ongoing union problems. Years before, I turned down the position of Director of Probation for New York State because I did not want to leave Massachusetts. In the end, I concluded that I was not qualified for the position of Commissioner. I didn't think that I was tough enough or suited to deal with the combination of difficult guards' unions, demanding inmate groups, management problems throughout the system of more than one dozen penal institutions, and being the subject of numerous lawsuits filed by inmates, staff, and advocacy groups. Moreover, the Commissioner was often the "whipping boy" of the media and the legislature. I was tempted to respond to the challenge, but I'm glad I did not.

I have reached for many stars since, but I have stayed within my own galaxy.

Almost Blown Away by Great-Granddad

I hope you have memories of Great-Granddad Art Wardwell. He was a former sea captain who spent over 30 years in the service. He was retired after taking the *Oceanographer*, a new U.S. Coast and Geodetic Survey ship, around the world. He passed away fifty years later at 104½ years old. Great-Granddad spent World War II on U.S. Navy minesweepers in the North Pacific, working in areas that the Japanese soldiers had abandoned after serious fighting. He brought back things left behind by Japanese soldiers. Swords, daggers, and two hand grenades have been kept at the farm in Vermont for the past 70 years. Great-Granddad told Grandma that the grenades were "duds" and not at all dangerous. He was so cautious that a child could not come into the barn when he was using a power tool, yet one of the hand grenades sat in the open in the barn and we used to pick it up and toss it around. You may have even handled a grenade in the barn.

I gave one of the hand grenades to a friend who was visiting from Massachusetts. He brought it home, but returned it at his wife's insistence, and I brought it back to Vermont. Last summer, our carpenter, David Mott, was working at the farmhouse and he saw one of the hand grenades. David, who is familiar with weapons, cautioned us that these things can become more dangerous over time and that we should turn them over to the State Police and, not only that, but that we should have the State Police come and get them. I did call and the State Police and National Guard came and took them away in a special container. The State Police officer later reported that they drilled a hole in each of the grenades and there was at least a trace of powder inside so they destroyed them.

I have often instructed a jury that the law requires them to weigh risk versus potential harm when assessing whether a person has a duty to act. In a way, the hand grenades are a classic illustration of that. The chances of the grenades being dangerous were very remote, yet if they exploded, the harm might be monumental.

One of our Japanese hand grenades

The Shot Heard 'Round Our World

When Grandma and I were first married, the family farmhouse in Chittenden was still fairly primitive. Built before 1830, it had a kitchen sink with a cold water tap only and an attached outhouse. We slept upstairs while Great-Granddad Art and Great-Grandma Evelyn slept downstairs.

One summer night, we were awakened by a blood-curdling scream followed a few minutes later by a gunshot from inside the house. We rushed downstairs and learned that Evelyn had gone to use the outhouse and when she picked up the seat cover, a porcupine stuck his nose up through the hole. Art loaded his rifle and shot the porcupine. Moments later we heard Evelyn shout that she was not coming back to the farm the next summer unless there was a bathroom. Sure enough, the next summer brought with it a bathroom complete with a toilet, sink, and bathtub, along with a hot water heater in the basement supplying hot water to the bathtub and the kitchen and bathroom sinks. It took almost another forty years for the installation of an upstairs bathroom in 2006.

When a new kitchen and pantry were added in 2013, things appeared pretty modern except there remains no heat other than a single wood-burning stove.

Great-Granddad Art was raised in the farmhouse with winter temperatures frequently dropping to 20 degrees below zero and but one stove to heat the house. In winter, his family kept the kitchen faucet running constantly to keep the water that came from a spring from freezing. The water still comes from the same spring, but we turn off the water and drain the pipes every year before the first freeze. When in high school, Great-Granddad boarded in Pittsford, ten miles away. He walked there from the farm Sunday evenings and he returned on foot Friday afternoons so that he could do his farm chores each weekend.

Great-Granddad Art lived to almost 105, so his hardships at the farm in his youth didn't seem to do him any harm.

Snubbing a High Holiday

On Monday, October 2, 1978, your dad was 9 and I was 39 years old. It was Rosh Hashanah and the Boston Red Sox and the New York Yankees had finished the regular season tied and were to play a single playoff game that day for the American League Eastern Division. I was in my second year as a District Court judge and had intended to attend Rosh Hashanah religious services that morning and watch the ballgame in the afternoon. However, I learned that the court system was in dire need of a judge for the Malden District Court. When asked if I could please sit there, I responded to the call for help and did not attend the religious services.

In court that afternoon, my court officer came to the side of the bench and whispered to me that the Yankee shortstop, Bucky Dent, had hit a three-run home run giving the Yankees a lead in the playoff game. Dent was not a power hitter as he averaged about three home runs per year. The Red Sox could not catch up, so this ended the Red Sox season. To this day, people in the Boston area refer to him as Bucky F'n Dent. As an avid Boston Red Sox fan, I wondered on the ride home if the Lord was punishing me for not attending High Holiday religious services.

Judge Ginsburg and I discuss issues such as these on our evening walks. If one performs a mitzvah (good deed) might he or she be rewarded here on earth or perhaps in the hereafter? Alternatively, if a person does something bad, might they suffer for it on earth, or in the hereafter? Was I punished for my snubbing Rosh Hashanah? If not, why was I not rewarded for performing the good deed of responding to a call for help?

Judge Ginsburg and I disagree on many things, but here we are in accord that doing a good deed adds to your self-satisfaction and to your reputation in the community and, from that, you will reap rewards for a lifetime. Doing wrong sullies your reputation and you will likely suffer as a result. Don't count on involvement from above.

An Honest Question

The defendant was charged with larceny over $250, meaning the government would have to prove both that he stole property from the expensive clothing store and that the property was worth more than $250. In such a case, if the government proves the theft, but the jury finds that the property was worth less than $250, then the defendant should be found guilty of petit larceny, a misdemeanor, rather than of grand larceny, a felony.

In this case, the jury deliberated for several hours and then sent me a note asking what would happen if they found that the defendant stole property worth exactly $250. In other words, was it the felony crime of larceny over $250 or the misdemeanor crime of larceny under $250? I carefully explained to the jury that, under the law, the defendant receives the benefit of any ambiguity in the law. Therefore, a person who steals something worth exactly $250 is guilty of larceny under $250.

The jury went back to deliberate and an hour later they found the defendant not guilty of both grand larceny and petit larceny.

I think they asked the question of me because someone on the jury was simply curious. I certainly hope they didn't misunderstand my instruction and conclude that one who steals something worth exactly $250 isn't guilty of anything. In retrospect, my instruction was probably ambiguous and I should have been more precise.

Cruising Down the River

In 1976, Cathy Moritz and Bob Wadsworth, John and Holly Cratsley, Steve Leonard and Judy Henry, and Grandma and I embarked on a multi-day canoe and camping trip on the Allagash River in Northern Maine. We covered almost 100 miles from the Churchill Dam to the town of Allagash. John and I had made the same trip with others the previous year. We relied on John's canoeing experience from his many years at the Beaver Camp for Boys as a camper and counselor.

When we reached a washed-out dam with quick-moving shallow water as well as exposed and hidden boulders, John and I agreed to demonstrate how it should be run. The others stood at the shore as John, in the stern, and I, in the bow, set out to conquer the spillway. One of the onlookers held an 8 mm camera. We got out in the current and approached the spillway intending to sweep around boulders. Somehow, we got sucked into a hole and struck a huge boulder sideways, bending, denting, and tearing the aluminum canoe. Ingloriously, we towed the canoe to shore only to watch the other six easily and safely navigate the spillway and boulder field.

We straightened out the canoe as best we could and then addressed the tear in the aluminum. John, who had taken on the name "Robinson" Cratsley, showed us how to extract pine pitch from trees and plug the holes in the aluminum. Our hands quickly became laden with sticky, smelly pine pitch that lingered for weeks, giving us a long-term remembrance of the trip.

Tens of friends and family members later viewed the film footage in an attempt to assess blame, either for the person in the bow who makes the short-term corrections or for the man in the stern who steers the vessel. No one blamed the river.

Washed-out Dam—Allagash River

Irrational Fear

Do you remember the story in *Bench Notes* about the burglar who hid in the bushes for a long time while the police and a dog searched the area and the man finally gave up when a policeman peed in the bushes on him? There may be a moral to the story if you consider it along with this.

Months after the arrest of the man in the bushes, I had before me in court a big strong man who had beaten and injured two people. I said that I was sentencing him to jail and he started crying. I later learned that he was afraid of mice and he had heard that there were lots of mice at the prison. I moved him to another facility. When I was a little boy, we lived in a six-family house where I had to go into the basement to put water into the water heater and there were rats in the basement. I carried a portable radio and sang out loud so that I wouldn't have to encounter a rat. I would have been horrified. Your dad lived in Washington, D.C., where there are rats and it never bothered him, although he is very wary of spiders.

I think the moral of these stories is that we all have our sensitivities and irrational fears. It's important to recognize them in other people, not to embarrass or take advantage of others, but to understand it's part of human fallibility. If you help or show understanding to a person with such a fear, that person will make you a friend for life.

A Dog of a Walk

Almost every night for decades, Judge Ginsburg and I would walk with one of his succession of small dogs, including Honey, Annie, and Pumpkin. It was good exercise for all of us. The dog was expected to do her business to avoid being taken out during the night. Once, we were walking Pumpkin and it started to rain pretty hard. We couldn't go home until the dog had done her business, which she refused to do. I kept reminding the dog that Judge Ginsburg and I spent every day telling people what to do and they did it, but this dog refused any such order while we got more and more soaked.

It wasn't until I dried off hours later that I realized that St. Francis of Assisi got it right:

Lord, grant me the strength to accept the things I cannot change, the courage to change the things I can, and wisdom to know the difference.

Grandpa's Art of Misplacing Things

Grandma sent me the poem "One Art" as a gentle reminder that I should be more careful. Your grandfather has a history of carelessness. Here are three examples.

As a high school student applying to college, I was required to write essays as to why I wanted to attend Tufts Engineering School, Worcester Polytech, and Rensselear Polytech. I carelessly sent one school an essay intended for one of the other schools. All three schools accepted me. Someone in the admissions office either had a sense of humor or really understood human frailty.

As a teenager, your dad spent two weeks with Uncle Bob and Aunt Judy at Long Beach Island in New Jersey. We met up with them in Connecticut to hand off your dad, and we had all of our luggage in our car from a trip to Canada. When they got to the shore, they discovered that I had put Grandma's suitcase in their car. Aunt Judy bought your dad clothing and said it was fun buying for a boy because she was used to buying only girls' clothing for her four daughters.

After playing tennis with a friend at Boston College, he drove me home. Hours later, I was unable to find my wallet. I went back to Boston College and didn't find it there. I called my friend's house and learned that his car was at the airport and he had left for a trip to Paris. I cancelled my credit cards and got a duplicate driver's license. Two weeks later, I found my wallet in my friend's car upon his return. The first stanza of "One Art" by Elizabeth Bishop sums it up:

"One Art"

The art of losing isn't hard to master;
so many things seem filled with the intent
to be lost that their loss is no disaster.

I Told You So

In *Bench Notes*, I described two incidents where members of ethnic minorities showed more empathy and understanding than one would expect in our society. You will remember that in one instance an African-American man who was the foreman at a muffler repair shop intervened and repaired my vehicle when it was apparent that I was having a very difficult time with David Chernoff in the waiting area. The foreman's boss was absolutely oblivious to my situation. Years later, David was in a McDonald's having lunch with a staff person from his special program and they were accompanied by an African-American teenager from the Boston area. Three wise-guy youths came into the restaurant and started to mock David publicly and the young man from Boston approached. He told them that David was his friend, what they were doing was very wrong, and if they did not leave immediately he would beat up all three of them in the parking lot. They left.

Grandma, Dhillon, your dad, and I drove to Vermont in early June so that your dad and I could run in a half marathon road race. It was raining in the Killington area when I got a flat tire. When we tried to change the tire we saw that our car jack was defective. I called for road service and was told that we would have to wait two hours. It was a Saturday afternoon and there was only one business open in the area, a high-end sporting equipment and clothing shop. I went through the store asking customers and staff if I could borrow a jack. Everyone with a car has a jack, yet every person I asked had an excuse why they could not help me. They were all Caucasians and appeared to be middle to upper class. I went back into the parking lot holding Dhillon's hand when I saw an African-American man getting into his car. I approached him, described our situation, and he, without hesitating, dug his jack from his car and told me to leave it next to the building and he would pick it up later.

I knew when I approached the man that he would help us. In my experience, people in minority groups generally show more compassion to people who need help. I don't know if it's because they better understand trouble and need. After changing the tire I suggested to Grandma that I leave some money with the jack as a "thank you gesture" and she said "no" because it might be construed as an insult. As they say, virtue is its own reward.

When I Married Carol

I had the real pleasure of performing the wedding, or solemnizing the marriage, of my close friends Carol Ball and Jim Re. Carol was a lawyer at the time and later became a Superior Court judge. Carol used to be an assistant district attorney in Middlesex County.

Shortly after I performed Carol's wedding, an older man named "Duke," who worked in the district attorney's office with Carol when she was a prosecutor, knocked on the door of my office at the Lowell Superior Court. He told me that he heard that I had married Carol Ball and he wanted me to know that Carol is one of the most wonderful persons he has ever met and that he was so glad that I married her. I thanked him very much for coming in to tell me that. As he left, he shook my hand and said, "I know that the two of you will be very happy together."

I was actually speechless. I just let him leave. I then called in my clerk, the late Brian Dunigan, and I told him that he had to do me a big favor. He had to track down the man from the district attorney's office and set him straight before the whole legal world started calling me to congratulate me on being married to Carol Ball. Carol and I have had great fun telling this story over the years.

Grandpa, He's Not a Bad Guy

Two local police officers stopped a car and found property taken from a recent housebreak. They arrested the defendant driver for receiving stolen property. After an evidentiary hearing, I ruled that the defendant's vehicle had been stopped illegally because the police had gone well beyond their legal jurisdiction by stopping the car well into a neighboring town when there was no hot pursuit. The defendant appeared pretty smug when I announced that, as a technical matter, the evidence could not be used against him and that he would go free.

I did not want the officers to feel embarrassed. I said in open court that I did not envy the police officers their dangerous work, especially when they stop and arrest felons in situations where the law makes the stop a close legal call. I also noted that they make these important calls under emergency situations without the benefit of legal advice.

When leaving the courthouse, one police officer was overheard telling the other officer that although he disagreed with my decision, "the judge is not a bad guy." That was one of the most meaningful complements I have ever received.

Without realizing it at the time, I was trying to stand in the shoes of the police officers to appreciate the situation from their vantage point. We should all do this more often.

Candy Is Dandy

I think it is important for the jury to know that they are appreciated and that the people who work for the courts really care about them. This is particularly important because most courthouses are not very comfortable or inviting places for private citizens.

Starting about fifteen years ago, I purchased individually wrapped hard candy for the jury. When they came back from a break or from lunch, they always found a hard candy on each juror's chair. I also had the court officers put a piece of candy on the chair of the prosecutor and defense attorney. When the case merited the attendance of members of the press, they found wrapped candy on their seats. I never acknowledged being the source of the treat, but I know it was well appreciated. Those few dollars that I spent on candy paid huge dividends in good will.

Little things mean a lot. They can make the difference in obtaining a job, finding a mate, and most other of life's endeavors.

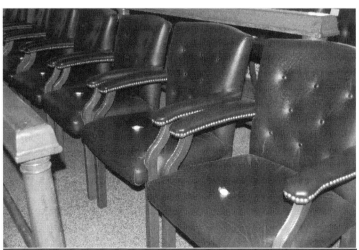

Lifesavers on jurors' seats in Lowell, Massachusetts

Don't Tell Me

I attended a laboratory tour and a two-day conference for judges, lawyers, and physicians at the Whitehead Institute in Cambridge, Massachusetts, where the DNA genome was mapped. It was fascinating to see pure DNA in the laboratory and to learn about the genetic similarities and differences among people. We learned how the study of genes can assist professionals in the criminal justice field apprehend the guilty and free the innocent. Also, the population as a whole can benefit through the prevention, detection, and treatment of diseases. We also learned that the study of one's genetic makeup could reveal whether an individual has a proclivity toward a particular disease.

When we learned that a blood test can determine whether a person is at a high risk for colon cancer, some people indicated that they would want to be tested so that if they were at a higher risk they could receive more frequent or earlier colonoscopies. Others indicated that they would not be tested because health insurers might try to raise their insurance rates if a test showed a higher risk of colon cancer.

We learned that a simple test can determine whether a person is at a higher risk for Alzheimer's disease. The speaker told us that all we had to do was spit in a cup during our morning coffee break and they would tell us the following morning the results of the Alzheimer's test using the genetic material in our saliva. There were almost 300 people at the lecture. Not one of us elected to learn whether we were at a higher risk of developing Alzheimer's disease. In my case, the decision had nothing to do with insurance rates. I think I just didn't want to know. On the one hand, if I had a higher risk, there is nothing I could do about it but worry and become depressed. On the other hand, it would help me plan for my family's future.

Technology is giving us the ability to do miraculous things, but many of us have not yet learned to what extent it may dictate our futures.

The Fortune Cookie

Years ago, upon completion of a murder trial, the jury was sequestered, which means they stayed overnight at a hotel after a day of deliberation. The purpose was to keep them away from outside trial publicity. They were with court officers who made sure the jurors had no contact with newspapers, television, radio, telephones, or computers.

The court officers loved to work with a sequestered jury because they received "comp time." Staying with a deliberating jury for three days could result in more than a week off later in the year for the court officers. When the state found it necessary to cut costs, sequestered juries were eliminated except for exceptionally public cases. The Dr. Greineder case, a murder trial over which I presided in 2001 and which was featured on Court TV, was one such case.

Years later, I was trying a murder case in Lowell concerning gang members and a drug sale that went bad. During the trial, one of my court officers kept trying to convince me that the case warranted a sequestered jury, which it didn't. Two or three times each day he asked me if the jury was going to be sequestered. Lunch was brought in each day for the jury because we did not want them eating lunch in local restaurants during the trial. One day, Chinese food was brought in for the jury. During the luncheon recess I retrieved a fortune cookie from the food delivery. I carefully removed the fortune paper and replaced it with a similar size note that I prepared on the computer and resealed the packet. I put the fortune cookie on the court officer's desk in the courtroom. I knew he would eat it.

During the trial in the afternoon the court officer was seated at his desk and I heard the cellophane wrapper from the fortune cookie being opened. He pulled out the fortune and it read, "This jury is not going to a hotel." He couldn't control himself and started to laugh so hard he had to leave the courtroom.

Sometimes you have to resort to humor to get your message understood.

Getting Used to It

In reflecting on the past, I have become more and more enamored with, and respectful of, the human condition. My class of officer trainees was assigned to the ship *Explorer* in Norfolk. As the designated most junior trainee, I was given the least desirable stateroom, the one farthest aft where the bulkhead was right next to the ship's propeller. At sea, the grinding noise was deafening for the first three days. After that, I didn't notice it at all and I found myself able to engage in conversations there in a normal tone of voice.

In a very serious personal injury case, the plaintiff sat in the courtroom in a wheelchair with his disability and discomfort on display for all to see for over a week. The defense attorney, Jay Lynch, a good friend and a great trial lawyer, later told me that the jury's verdict clearly evidenced that they had gotten too used to, and were almost comfortable with, the plaintiff's injuries. Jay felt the plaintiff would have fared much better had he been in the courtroom for his testimony only.

Forgetting About It

Nature helps us forget difficult experiences and leads us back to normalcy. I must have suffered in the aftermath of my aortic valve replacement surgery, especially because a complication caused my return to the hospital for another procedure. However, it didn't take long for me to become almost nostalgic about the operation when I remembered the events as being almost pleasant. A year later, I advised a state Supreme Judicial Court judge who was about to undergo the same procedure that it was "a piece of cake."

Two years, ago, your dad and I ran the early June Covered Bridges Half Marathon through Woodstock, Vermont. At mile eleven, my feet were killing me. At mile twelve, heat exhaustion added to my agony as I kept repeating to myself, "never again, never again." After crossing the finish line, I embraced your dad, picked up my race t-shirt, and by the time we reached the beverage/snack tent, we were talking about doing it again. We did run it the next year. Bob Lebowitz and I can personally attest to the fact that marathon runners who suffer the agonizing final eight miles after "hitting the wall" at eighteen miles forget the pain rather quickly.

I remember a female physician testifying at a trial that the greatest pain known to women is childbirth and that not many mothers would bear more than one child if the painful memory of an earlier birth did not substantially subside.

It's really true that "sunshine follows the rain" and it's best to let nature help us leave the hard times in the past.

Covered Bridges Half Marathon
Grandpa wearing bib no. 340

Let It Snow

Some eligible people try to avoid jury duty and most people who are summoned hope they will not be selected. However, once people are selected to serve, their attitude quickly changes as they realize they are part of a decisional process that directly affects the well-being of other people.

I was presiding over a very interesting civil case in Lowell involving the diagnosis and treatment of prostate cancer. The fourteen members of the jury gave their full attention to the expert witnesses including physicians and scientists who expressed different views on the subject at hand. It was mid-January and the snow started to fall before noon. Each day, we had found a convenient quitting time to be around 4:00 to 4:15 P.M. When it was 2:30 P.M., I noticed that several inches of snow had already fallen and learned that several more were expected before evening. I interrupted a witness and told the jury that I knew that most of them lived more than 20 miles away and that the Lowell Connector, the road from the city to the highway, was not always well maintained during a snow storm. I suggested that we quit early and resume in the morning. Each one of the jurors looked at me, some shook their heads back and forth while the others said "no." We continued with the witness until 4:15. One of the jurors told the court officer at the end of the day that it was like reading a good book and they were not about to put it down. Incidentally, the witness was very grateful that he could finish his testimony that day.

The general public is often seen as being cynical when it comes to the court system. Our greatest fans are those who have served as jurors. Every juror and every judge learns something each day that they didn't know before coming to court.

Do You Want Fairness or Justice?

Rayan, suppose you did something wrong and your mom told you that you were not going to get to go to a sleepover at a friend's house. You complained to Mom that when your younger brother Dhillon had done the same thing, he only received a timeout in his room, and that your younger sister LeeLee received only a scolding for the same misconduct. Suppose your mom responded by saying that she did what she felt was correct and that Dhillon, LeeLee, and you are different people. You and your mom may not have realized it, but the two of you were engaging in a discussion that goes to the very heart of the criminal justice system. You were saying that you were treated *unfairly* while Mom was saying that she had reached a *just* result with each of the three of you. Punishment can be meted out fairly or justly, but often not both, as you saw in your case.

I can see why the public gets angry when one judge sentences a person to probation while another judge sentences a similar person who has committed a similar crime to a significant period in jail. Each judge had a different view of what justice required. In deciding whether a person should be sentenced to jail, judges often weigh four traditional factors: (1) whether the person is a danger to himself or others; (2) whether prison for this person would deter others in the community from committing a crime; (3) whether the misdeed was such that it cries out for severe punishment; and (4) whether prison is the only place where the person can receive appropriate treatment.

Sometimes the law compels me to disregard the four factors and send a person to jail even when I feel that jail is not appropriate. This happens because the law for the particular crime mandated a specific minimum jail term. Such laws treat similar people similarly and are, by definition, fair but not necessarily just.

So, Rayan, I think some people would agree with your plea for fairness while others would agree with your mom's view that justice should prevail.

Highpointers

Repetitive minor irritations can sometimes be far more disturbing than a single major one. In the courtroom, I can deal with an act of misbehavior or disrespect, but I can be driven to distraction by a person who repeatedly irritates me. For example, when a lawyer repeatedly points his index finger at me when speaking, I am really irritated and I think of Jerimoth Hill.

The Highpointers Club is a nationwide organization whose members strive to visit the highest point of every state. My law school classmate Harry Dickerson belongs to the Highpointers and Grandma and I escorted him to the high points of Connecticut (Mt. Frissell), Massachusetts (Mt. Greylock), New York (Mt. Marcy), and Vermont (Mt. Mansfield). Harry was then going to drive his car to summit Jerimoth Hill, the highest point in Rhode Island at an elevation of 812 feet.

Jerimoth Hill is located in rural Rhode Island. The property owner lived in a house on the property. A dirt path, not far from his house, extended from the road to Jerimoth Hill. This man would sit on his porch while car after car from all over the country would park near his house and Highpointers would walk the short distance to Jerimoth Hill. This minor repetitive irritant exasperated him. He tried a "No Trespassing" sign, which was ignored. Then came larger signs, a loud speaker, and video cameras, all to no avail. He became even more desperate and tried personal confrontations, threats, physical assaults, and finally firing his shotgun over hikers' heads. The landowner told the Highpointer leader that he would let them visit on certain federal holidays, but people coming from far and wide would not abide by this. Finally, the man sold the property to the state. It leased Jerimoth Hill to Brown University and it is now a state park, accessible to all.

See what I mean about the cumulative effect of minor irritants?

You Know Me

"Car Talk" was a nationwide call-in NPR radio show that aired every Saturday from 1977 to 2012 and now we hear reruns every weekend. Tom and Ray Magliozzi owned the Good News Garage in Cambridge, Massachusetts, and they were known as "Click and Clack, the Tappet Brothers." They gave advice to people who called in and described problems with their cars. Tom and Ray used self-deprecating humor and kidded with those who called in for advice. Click and Clack made public appearances and gave performances in support of charities. They claimed to be represented by the imaginary law firm of Dewey, Cheetham, & Howe (phonetically, "Do we cheat 'em and how"). There was a sign for the law firm in their office window overlooking Harvard Square. Grandma and I often listened to them when in the car. We have always thought that everyone, especially in the Boston area, knows of "Click and Clack, the Tappet Brothers."

I was selecting a jury in Dedham on a case involving an auto repair. The plaintiff's attorney retained Ray Magliozzi as his expert witness, who would testify that the defendant auto shop negligently repaired the vehicle causing great harm.

Since, in my eyes, the prospective expert witness was a real celebrity, I decided to ask the entire jury panel, from which the jury would be selected, if they knew of Ray Magliozzi, the "Good News Garage," the "Tappet Brothers," or NPR's "Car Talk." Of the 55 prospective jurors in the room, only two raised their hands. On further inquiry, only one of them had ever heard of the witness. After the jury was selected and the plaintiff presented its case, I saw Ray Magliozzi as he was leaving the courthouse. I invited him into my office and asked him if he was going to tell his listeners that, out of a random group of 55 citizens, only one had ever heard of him. He is a nice, self-effacing gentleman who smiled and replied, "Probably not."

Harvard Square Office of Dewey Cheetham & Howe

Up Close and Personal

"The first thing we do, let's kill all the lawyers"[2] is one of the most quoted lines in Shakespeare's works. However, Shakespeare was promoting rather than demeaning lawyers. The line was uttered by a rebel to the crown who wanted to tear down order and promote worship of the rebel chief. He knew that those trained in the law would not abide by this. Over the centuries, the cynical public has ignored the context of the statement and instead has chosen to see it as a blanket condemnation of lawyers and the legal profession.

Recently, on NPR's humorous call-in radio program "Car Talk," it was noted that a national survey regarding public approval of various professions rated lawyers with an approval rate of 17%. This was between car salesmen at 9% and auto mechanics at 22%. Your dad attributes this to a frustrated public lashing out at impersonal institutions like Congress and the legal profession. Most people hate Congress yet approve of their own congressperson. The public may demean the legal profession when it reads about a suspect who "lawyers up" or about a lawyer who represents a very unpopular client accused of horrendous acts or is affiliated with a detested cause.

Many people do not have a high regard for the court system. I've heard people demean it by calling it political, inefficient, and rife with unqualified hacks and lazy workers. This is sometimes reinforced by how it's portrayed in the popular media. Yet, the biggest promoters of the courts are the people who have served as jurors because they have seen justice firsthand and have gotten to know the people who administer and facilitate it. When summoned for jury duty, many people express a desire to avoid jury service perhaps because of a disrespect for the system, but I can vouch that once jurors are sitting on a case, they unanimously feel that the judge, court staff, and attorneys are beyond reproach and that they are proud to participate in a system that works.

When you think of it, that's how we feel about our postman, auto mechanic, and car salesman. We become much less cynical with personal involvement.

---

[2] William Shakespeare, *Henry the Sixth*, part II, act IV, scene ii.

Does Valentine Rhyme with Title IX?[3]

For thirty-five years, I have purchased two to three dozen red tulips on Valentine's Day and brought them to my assigned courthouse. I give a tulip to each and every female I encounter in the courthouse. This includes the judges, clerks, court officers, jurors, probation officers, administrative assistants, law librarians, court reporters, and the attorneys appearing in my session.

My celebration of Valentine's Day at the court has been appreciated by the recipients of the tulips and commented upon favorably by others; that is, until last year. Two male court employees commented to the clerk that my practice was inappropriate in today's world of both gender equality and gay rights. When my clerk told me of this, my first reaction was "get a life."

Now, one year later as I bought red tulips for the females at the court, I realized that it may be a more complicated issue. Many have made sacrifices for religious, racial, gender, and sexual preference equality in the workplace. But there are other areas such as expressing appreciation and affection with flowers that do not call for absolute equality. Blind obedience to political correctness can destroy appropriate warmth and feeling toward others.

---

[3] Title IX of the Education Amendments Act of 1972 outlaws sex discrimination and classification based on gender in schools receiving federal financial support.

Drawing Inferences

Dhillon, if you were to come downstairs a little late one morning and see that Rayan's backpack was not on the floor in its usual place, you might conclude that he had already left the house because he always takes his backpack with his books and lunch in it to school. LeeLee, if you looked out your bedroom window in the morning and you saw Miss Melissa outside wearing a heavy coat, a hat, and gloves, you might conclude that it was very cold outside. Rayan, if you walked home from the school bus stop and saw you dad's car in the driveway, you might conclude that he was home early.

All three of you would be drawing reasonable inferences, based upon information known to you and your experience in this world. However, it is possible that you were each wrong. What if Rayan was really in the basement with his backpack or if Miss Melissa was coming to show your mom her new coat, hat, and gloves, or perhaps, your dad swapped cars with your mom and he was still at work with her car? Most of the time people are correct when they draw reasonable inferences. That happens a lot in court. If no one saw a thief steal candy from the store, but someone saw a man eating that candy a short time later near the store, one could draw the inference that he was the thief.

When I instruct a jury, I tell them that they can draw reasonable inferences, but they cannot speculate or guess. As an example, I tell jurors that I am a jogger and I know that my next door neighbor is an early riser. If I run in late morning and see a newspaper in my neighbor's driveway, I usually draw the inference that my neighbor is away. That's a reasonable inference, but there is a chance that the neighbor is ill or is sleeping late or just forgot about the newspaper that day.

It's fun to think about whether you are drawing an inference or relying on direct information when you draw a conclusion. For example, if there is no one at my usually crowded commuter train stop when I arrive, I usually draw the inference that I have just missed the train. But sometimes when I arrive, I think that I can see the red taillight of a train far down the track. Then, based on a direct observation rather than an inference, I can conclude that I have just missed the train.

Kids in the Jury Pool

We have a one day–one trial jury system in Massachusetts. In such a system a person serves on no more than one case and if they are not selected for a case, then they may leave. That concludes their jury duty for at least three years. Jurors are randomly selected from the names in the annual census. However, anyone called for jury duty can defer service to another date, one that they select. This results in a tremendous influx of young jurors during the month of May. This is because thousands of college students defer their jury service until sometime in May, between their last final exam and the start of their summer activity.

I have presided over trials in May when the vast majority of a twelve-person jury is comprised of jurors under the age of 22. There may be no credible studies on the impact of young jurors on the system, but trial lawyers do have anecdotal evidence that is quite interesting. Civil attorneys say that young jurors are generally favorable toward plaintiffs. They also say that college-age jurors do not fully appreciate the value of money and their awards are relatively meager. To a college student, $50,000 seems like a lot of money, yet it might be totally inadequate to compensate a person with a lifetime disability. Criminal attorneys say that college-age jurors are less likely to accept the testimony of police officers, but they favor law enforcement when it comes to child abuse cases.

I have heard many respected people say that people often are liberal when young, middle-of-the-road in middle age, and conservative as seniors. I wonder if that would be confirmed in a person's performance as a juror.

Scent and Sensibility

The defendant was on trial for selling drugs to an undercover police officer. One of the jurors was sight-impaired and was accompanied by a large German shepherd dog trained to assist him outside his home. The juror was seated at the end of the first row of jurors close to the witness stand. For the entire trial, the dog lay on the courtroom floor right in front of the juror. I could tell that the dog was very sensitive to his environs because he lifted his head and stared at everyone who moved or spoke.

The case against the defendant was very strong as the undercover officer testified that he actually bought drugs from the defendant in exchange for money. Two other police officers testified that they observed the drug transaction from a distance and when they arrested the defendant minutes later, the defendant had, in his possession, money that they had marked with small ink dots before the drug sale. The defendant elected to testify in his own behalf and he told a preposterous story about receiving the marked money from someone he had given change to. The dog stared at him when he told this to the jury and I thought the dog was going to bark at him. Later, when he left the witness stand and walked within inches of the dog, I wondered if the dog might bite him. I'm sure the dog was evaluating all of the witnesses at some level.

The jury's verdict of guilty took a bite out of the defendant while the well-trained dog just watched.

Until Death Do Us Part Ceremonies

When I was Chairman of the Parole Board I obtained a Justice of the Peace Commission to help facilitate the extradition of our parolees who got into trouble in other states. I opted to have the Commission include the power to solemnize marriages. I do not perform many marriages, perhaps two or three each year, but over forty years, I have performed well over one hundred marriages. I performed the wedding of your cousins Barbara and Geoff Chupp, Jeffrey and Nancy Spector, and Sarah and Nat Dailey. I have performed the wedding of some of my colleagues including Judge Carol Ball, Judge Jeffrey Locke, and Lenny and Vivian Kesten.

I live in Newton, which has substantial Jewish and Catholic populations. In Newton, there are many interfaith couples and, unfortunately, neither the local rabbis nor the priests will perform an interfaith marriage ceremony. I remember performing a wedding at a university's faculty club where the rabbi recited a prayer in Hebrew and the priest a prayer in Latin and I tied the knot in English. The father of the bride was the president of a temple and the parents of the groom were leaders in their church. I was so disappointed that religion was an impediment rather than a help to these families.

A marriage certificate must contain the address of the ceremony. I performed two weddings on boats in Boston Harbor. The address I reported was the boat's location in latitude and longitude at the time I pronounced the couple married. I performed a wedding on a beach and reported the address of #1 Beach Road after the official at town hall agreed we could make up that address.

A justice of the peace is permitted to charge a wedding fee. I have never done so. If people insist, I suggest that they make a contribution to an organization that helps disabled people. When I decline a fee, I usually remark that this commitment is the one life sentence that I enjoy imposing.

Until Death Do Us Part Probationer

It was 4 P.M. on a Friday and a probationer was brought before me in custody with handcuffs. The probation officer told me that the man had done well on probation for two years, but that a blood or urine test had shown that he had consumed an illegal drug. It was neither cocaine nor heroin, but it may have been an ingredient in an unauthorized pain-relieving medication. The probation officer told me that he wanted the man held in custody for a few days in order "to give him religion." You may remember how I dislike that term.

A woman who was listening intently sat in the courtroom and I asked her if she had an interest in the defendant. She told me that they had been married and they had had a pretty good marriage but that they broke up when she moved to Florida. She had come back to Massachusetts for medical treatment and she planned on staying. She also said that she and the defendant had gotten back together and they wanted to re-marry on Monday morning but couldn't because he was in custody and they couldn't find anyone to perform the ceremony. I learned from the probation officer that the probationer had been living with his mother and was working.

I ordered him released and to stay at his mother's home. I told him and his former wife that they could go to City Hall on Monday morning at 8:30 to apply for a marriage license, and then proceed to the District Court and ask the judge to waive the three-day waiting period. If they did this, then they could return to my courtroom and I would perform the marriage. They left and I figured there was little chance I would see them again.

On Monday at 10 A.M. they both appeared in my courtroom with license in hand. I performed the wedding and the court reporter gave them a transcript of the ceremony. I think that this good deed is working out. The probation officer told me months later that everyone was doing well. I was so pleased.

A Nuclear Reaction

I had the honor of being invited by a group of Japanese judges, lawyers, and law professors to meetings of the Osaka Bar Association in Japan to discuss the American jury system and how it might work in Japan. Grandma accompanied me on the trip and we found our Japanese hosts to be very hospitable.

We attended a private reception at the bar association where everyone was very nice to us until an elderly lawyer approached me and told me that he lived in Japan during the Second World War and he personally saw what America did to his people by exploding the nuclear bombs over Hiroshima and Nagasaki, which caused death and serious injury to hundreds of thousands of Japanese people. He went on to berate me and blame me for what he said were the sins of my fathers. All I could tell him was that I was a very small child at the time and should not be held responsible. I don't know if I was able to say that I was opposed to the use of nuclear weapons. The people who invited me to Osaka were very embarrassed and they told me that the old man was drunk and a bit crazy. I told them not to worry and that I understood the situation. A bit later, perhaps the next day, the old man presented Grandma and me with a small gift.

In retrospect, I feel good that I served as a catharsis for this man who, contrary to his culture of no confrontation, felt he needed to do what he did. I may well have felt the same way if our situations were reversed and I wonder if I would have spoken out the way he did.

Feeling the Past

In his poem "Directive," Robert Frost takes us to a rural mountainous area of Vermont where there had been a town, a farm, and a house that no longer exist. Thousands of years before, the ice receded there, yet one could still feel "a certain coolness this side of Panther Mountain." Can't we all sometimes feel that something has happened in a place although we see no present sign of it?

I have entered empty courtrooms the day after an important trial concluded and felt some remnant of it although everything was in its place and ready for the new day's work.

Years ago there was a tragic bus accident in Canada where several school-age children were killed, including four children from our community in Newton, Massachusetts. On Sunday afternoon there was a memorial service at our Temple for the children. It was very well attended and certainly there was an outpouring of emotion during the service. I was not in attendance and did not know of the service that day.

That evening, we attended a music program in the same sanctuary as the afternoon memorial service. We arrived very early and took a seat inside the nearly vacant sanctuary. I was overwhelmed with the feeling that something significant had recently occurred there, even though there were no outward signs of it.

I wonder whether we human beings are able to discern almost invisible signs of past events or whether we do indeed have a sixth sense of past events.

One Downside of Our Electronic World

Before the age of smartphones, it was relatively easy to insure that jurors decided the case only on what was learned at trial. A jury that was deliberating on a manslaughter case had not reached a decision the previous day and was returning to continue deliberations in the morning. The court officer reported to me that a juror had arrived with the *Encyclopaedia Britannica*, prepared to read the definition of "manslaughter" to the other jurors. This would have been inappropriate because different jurisdictions used different definitions of manslaughter. Because the juror had studied the book the previous evening, I replaced him with an alternate juror.

Fast forward to the present. All jurors have the capability of seeking a definition of manslaughter at home, at the courthouse, or in transit. We judges instruct jurors that they are not to perform their own investigation during the case, such as going to the scene or conducting any research on any of the people involved in the case or any issue of law. We allow jurors to take notes during the trial. If a juror is permitted to use an electronic tablet for note taking, it would be very difficult to make sure they don't access outside information.

To me, the only thing that works, or mostly works, is peer pressure. If one juror sees another juror disobeying the judge's instruction, that juror will probably first caution the other juror and then report the action to a court official if need be. I fear that a juror can do a pretty intensive search on the Internet and come up with information on the lawyers, the judge, the parties, and the witnesses. Imagine if someone researched the criminal defendant during a trial and found a treasure trove of newspaper articles describing his conduct over the years or, even worse, if they found out something horrible about a person with the same name and they didn't realize it was a different person.

This situation is unlikely to improve with the advent of more sophisticated electronics and I suppose it is likely to worsen. Some judges appoint the foreperson at the start rather than at the end of the trial and put the responsibility on the foreperson to insure that no jurors do electronic research while in the jury room or courtroom. That looks like a positive approach.

What's Missing in the Picture

The late Judge Robert Bohn was one of my closest friends. We served together on the Parole Board and the Superior Court and we went on many canoeing and backpacking ventures together. I went with him to the hospital when he received cancer treatments and toward the end I used to spend evenings with him at his house helping him complete his court work.

After Judge Bohn died, I joined some other friends and family of his in arranging to have a portrait painted of him from a number of photographs. When the portrait was completed and shipped from California, we arranged for a portrait hanging at the Essex Superior Court in Salem where he served as the administrative judge for many years. Friends, family, fellow judges, and lawyers attended the portrait hanging ceremony and I served as the photographer. When *Lawyers Weekly* decided to devote two pages to pictures of the event, I sent them electronic copies of all of my photographs. I was not in a single photo. Several people who saw the photo exhibition in the newspaper and noted my absence in the display commented that Judge Bohn and I must have had a falling out at the end. The reason that I was not in any photos was because I had taken them all.

It is so important to think about more than the present moment. Had I done so, I would have avoided an embarrassment.

Known by the Company You Keep

Prisoners who are associated with organized crime are generally the most well-behaved inmates in prison and they can add a real sense of order to a penal institution. Although they may be known as "heavy hitters," they usually earn the trust of the prison administration and often end up as trustees and work in minimum security assignments such as lawn care and gardening outside the prison gates. When I was Chairman of the Parole Board, I would talk very cordially with these people when I arrived for the monthly parole hearings. Most of them were about my age. Now, they are in the community having either served their sentences or having been released for legal reasons. Some now reside in Boston's North End.

After a judicial educational conference in Boston, I walked with a group of judges to a North End restaurant for dinner in celebration of the birthday of one of my colleagues. As we entered the restaurant, we passed a group of about six senior citizens and we recognized one another. I had met them time and time again while they were gardening outside the penal institutions. They greeted me by name like an honored judicial guest. I shook their extended hands as I passed and many of my colleagues stared in disbelief. I had to explain in a whisper at the table.

In the Doghouse

I was sitting in a civil session of the Superior Court in Middlesex County one afternoon when a case was called and both attorneys came forward to be heard on a motion. One of the lawyers told me that he was unable to file a memorandum in advance of the hearing because he was engaged in Norfolk County before Judge Elizabeth Butler. I immediately knew that he was not telling me the truth. I told him that he must be mistaken about the name of the judge because she was away and that my wife and I were dog sitting for Willy, her large black Gordon setter. Maybe I was too kind to the lawyer, but he got the message as did everyone else in the courtroom, and I don't think that he will lie to a judge again.

A person can destroy his professional and personal reputation in the blink of an eye. Time and time again we see that the cover-up is worse than the misdeed and presidents, governors, and others never seem to learn and continue to pay the price. Don't you.

A Gordon Setter

Willy Again

Willy, the wonderful Gordon setter, belonged to a Superior Court judge and her husband Jim, who was a practicing lawyer. I had been asked if we could take Willy for a few days because they were going away and I indicated that I would clear it with Grandma. A day later I was sitting in a civil motions session of the Superior Court and I saw that Jim was the attorney on the next motion. I called both lawyers up to the sidebar and disclosed my relationship with Jim's family that included the dog. I said that I could decide the motion fairly, but I would send the case to another judge if either of the lawyers felt uncomfortable with me hearing the motion. Both lawyers, after consulting with their respective clients, agreed that I could hear the motion.

After the motions hearing I took a short recess and called home. When I returned to the courtroom, I brought the lawyers back up to the bench where I stated the following to Jim, "Counsel, I have good news and bad news for you. The good news is that I called home and we can take Willy for a few days. The bad news is that you have lost the motion."

Down, But Not Out

I was in academic trouble after the end of my second year at Tufts. I withdrew for a year and attended another school in the interim. When I returned to Tufts, I made a comeback and graduated with honors. Two professors, Fred Nelson and Kenneth Astill, helped put me on the right track and I am eternally grateful to them for recognizing my potential when others may have had their doubts.

During my tenure as a Superior Court judge, I have guided a number of judicial interns. Many came from the top of their class at premier colleges. I also welcomed persons who were struggling academically and/or needed direction and inspiration. I could see myself in some of them and have enjoyed learning about their subsequent successes.

To mention just a few, I remember a young man who had only fair success at a little-known college. As my intern, I put him to work on a team that included the clerk, court officer, and law clerk. He developed a sense of confidence in himself as well as a career direction. He excelled in law school, clerked for the Supreme Judicial Court, as a legal scholar authored a popular practice book for lawyers, and he is currently supervising in-house counsel for a major corporation. Another intern who totally lacked direction at the beginning absolutely caught fire, succeeded in law school, and is currently doing quite well in the private practice of law.

Most of us stumble at some point in our lives and the challenge is to pick ourselves up and help others do the same. The rewards are great. I am very proud of the accomplishments of all of my interns, especially those who needed help at the beginning.

I'd Like to Pardon You

The judge in a jury trial has the responsibility of choosing the foreperson of the jury. During a trial, I study the jury questionnaires and also observe each juror's level of attentiveness. In a recent civil case, I reviewed the questionnaire from a 68-year-old juror who disclosed that he was ashamed to admit that fifty years before he had been convicted of the misdemeanor crime of "Illegitimacy." In those days, the unmarried father of a child was charged criminally to insure that he paid child support. My juror had been convicted at age 18, had been in no further trouble for 50 years, and he still felt like a second-class citizen. I appointed him foreperson of the jury.

After the jury returned a perfectly appropriate verdict, the foreperson asked to speak to me privately. He said, "Judge, you don't know how important it is to me that you selected me as the foreman of the jury." I said, "Of course I know, and that's why I appointed you." I then told him how he could petition the court to seal his record. It's too bad that courts can't pardon individuals, that's for the executive.

I don't know which of us felt better afterward. I do worry that, through inadvertence, I have missed many opportunities to help other people.

Parents Can Do Dumb Things, Too

On a Monday morning I was presiding over drug cases at the Brockton Superior Court. When walking in the public corridor from my chambers to the clerk's office, I passed a bench outside of a courtroom. A mother was sitting on the bench screaming at her little girl for playing with her sippy cup and spilling some juice. Given the minor misdeed, the mother's behavior was over the top and she struck me as someone who had behavioral problems herself.

Last week, my close friend Dr. Michelle Silvera, who is a pediatric neuroradiologist, shared a story over dinner. At the Boston Children's Hospital, parents who escort their child into the magnetic imaging room are required to sign twice that they are not carrying or wearing anything metallic because the magnetic field in the room is very strong and cannot be turned off. On the previous Saturday, a child's father signed the two forms and walked into the MRI room. Suddenly, he was thrown across the room as if by invisible hands and he ended up with his back pinned against the MRI machine. It turned out that he was an off-duty Boston Police Officer and he carried a gun in a rear holster. It was very difficult to extricate him from the machine. The hospital security staff was fearful that the strong magnet might have released the safety device on the gun.

That father was careless and could have endangered others. I wondered how he could or would go about disciplining his own child in the future given his own reckless action.

Grandpa on the MTA

Since retiring as a full-time judge, I have been working two days per week with a law firm in Boston. I take the subway train from Newton to Boston and it is very convenient. On my return commute to Newton, the seats are usually taken and I stand for the thirty-minute trip. Sometimes a seated person on the train will offer their seat to me and I always decline.

What is so interesting is that only women have offered me their seats. There are always young men seated and they are usually involved with their smartphones. Sometimes I see an elderly person or a disabled person standing and I suggest to a seated male that he should give up his seat and he does.

When I have described my experience on public transit to Grandma and other women, I have been advised that many men are not good at multi-tasking and that they might well be oblivious to the needs of another if they are engaged in reading, but that most women are natural multi-taskers who are aware of their total environment.

Your dad tells me it's purely cultural and that in Russia, young men are expected to give up their seats not only to senior citizens, but also to women of any age and to small children. Ask him about the time on the St. Petersburg Metro when he failed to give his seat to a healthy looking little boy and was painfully punished by the mother, who stepped on his dress shoe with a well-placed high heel.

Last week, the first male in two years offered me his seat. He appeared disabled with Parkinson's disease and, of course, I declined his offer.

Carrying a Big Stick

President Theodore Roosevelt's enlightened foreign policy was to "speak softly and carry a big stick." The big stick that judges carry is the power to hold people in contempt for not obeying a court order or for misbehaving in the courtroom. If held in contempt of court, the offender could receive a fine, be sent to jail, or both.

Unfortunately, there are a few judges in both the state and federal courts who do not have an enlightened judicial policy. They rely on the big stick to enforce their authority. To me, overuse of the contempt power only shows the judge to be a bully. It does not win the judge the respect he or she seeks, nor does it ensure obedience to orders and good conduct in the courtroom.

After warning a lawyer multiple times that he was inappropriately badgering the witness, I called the attorneys to the sidebar and told the offending lawyer that I had been a judge for thirty-five years and had never held anyone in contempt. I implored him not to be the first. It would not only constitute an indelible stigma on his reputation, it might also result in a fine and/or imprisonment. Fortunately for him, he changed course and became almost civil.

I am proud of the fact that I have not held anyone in contempt. When giving a talk on civility at a bar association meeting, I jokingly said that that was because I had two vicious Dobermans placed in the courtroom.

The key in the courtroom and in life is to develop a sense of knowing when and where trouble is brewing and how to head it off civilly, that is, without a stick. When your dad was a teenager, he, Grandma, and I took Tae Kwon Do lessons where the students learned hand, kick, and stick fighting. I remember learning that the goal was never to have to use any of it.

Taken to the Cleaners

The expression "taken to the cleaners" is used when a person is cheated out of something or is taken advantage of.

The Corner Cleaners is located next to the Newton District Court on busy Washington Street. Often, it is impossible to find nearby parking in the area. Recently, seeing no available space, I parked ahead of the last meter by the front of the shop and ran into the dry cleaners carrying a suit. When I returned to my car a few minutes later, I found a $20 ticket on the windshield. The police officer had appeared and disappeared in a flash.

The police have a difficult job in the community. They need to gain the cooperation of the citizenry by establishing themselves as both protectors and helpers. Sometimes, this means letting people off with a verbal warning or sometimes simply doing nothing. I don't know if the officer saw me, but if so, he or she would have seen that I was a senior citizen who couldn't find a parking space and would not be parked for more than a minute or two. No law enforcement purpose was served and the ticket only alienated a citizen who has supported the police for forty years.

Many communities post a hidden policeman with a radar gun at the bottom of steep hills to hand out $50 to $100 speeding tickets to motorists. There is no valid law enforcement purpose for ticketing almost every car that descends the hill when even the most cautious drivers will tend to exceed the speed limit. A common explanation is that this is done to raise extra revenue for the local government. Isn't the role of the police to fight crime and help people and not to raise money for the municipality? Should they really wonder why many law-abiding people do not respect them? They should be told that the citizenry does not enjoy being taken to the cleaners.

Orr Is Golden

Almost every hockey fan would agree that the greatest hockey player of all time was Bobby Orr. He was faster, more nimble, and smarter than all others playing the game. He played for the Boston Bruins for most of his career and he is a sports icon here in hockey, as Bill Russell is in basketball, Ted Williams is in baseball, and Tom Brady is in football. Bobby Orr stands out above most sports heroes because he is also what is known in Yiddish as a "mensch," that is, he is a real human being.

Bobby Orr has devoted his years after hockey to helping others. He does it in a low-key way because he does not seek recognition from the press, his fans, or even from the people whom he helps. I can give you a personal example that makes me cry. A judge friend of mine lost his wife to cancer last year. His wife grew up in Boston when Bobby Orr played hockey here and he was her childhood hero. She attended Bruins games and had posters of Bobby Orr in her room. She knew all of the statistics that memorialize his hockey achievements.

Last year, as she was in her last days at the Massachusetts General Hospital, Bobby Orr appeared in her hospital room and sat and talked with her about the Bruins of her childhood and her favorite games and players. They reminisced and he put a poster on her wall and gave her other memorabilia. After they discussed her childhood memories, Bobby Orr left and, as usual, there was no fanfare about this "mitzvah."

I learned later that a clerk at the court where my colleague sits knew of the woman's plight and also knew someone who knew Bobby Orr. He also knew that Bobby Orr is a rare person who puts others ahead of himself.

Judging Grandpa

The expression "No taste pleases all palates" refers to more than people's food preferences. It applies to taste in movies, books, and most important, other people. We are all liked, even loved, by some people while there are others who may dislike us or even hate us.

I try every day to be respected by everyone including the lawyers, court staff, and jurors. I do not raise my voice or speak in a threatening or demeaning tone, and I try to explain why I am making a particular ruling. However, I am always taken aback when I receive my periodic judicial evaluations.

The Judicial Performance Evaluation is a confidential survey of attorneys, jurors, and court staff. One part rates the judge numerically on characteristics such as patience, attentiveness, preparation, respect, promptness, control of courtroom, fairness, lack of bias, and arrogance. A judge with a low score is required to receive special training.

The most interesting part of the evaluation is the comments people make about the judge. Most comments about Superior Court judges are positive although we all receive negative ones. In my last evaluation, there were 215 attorneys, 21 court employees, and 15 jurors who responded. To show the diversity in views, I am listing an equal number of positive and negative comments. It's hard to believe they're all talking about the same person.

He is the best judge in the Superior Court.

Despite years as a Judge, he has a limited understanding of the law.

First rate in every respect: intelligent, industrious, modest, fair-minded and very pleasant to work with. Can't ask for more.

His trials are more like circuses than legal proceedings.

Judge is a sensitive kind man who brings judicial temperament and compassion to the bench.

He is short to the point of rudeness with attorneys.

Judge is a model justice, knowledgeable, respectful, fair and funny.

Judge is notoriously lenient and does not seem at all concerned with having such a reputation.

Your Reputation

As a senior judge, I am often called upon to make presentations to newer judges. I think that my most important message deals with acquiring and keeping a good reputation. I start my lectures with my theory that if a judge conducts himself or herself in a manner that causes others to perceive that the judge is a good person, is a person who wants to do the right thing, and is a person who can be trusted, then that judge is essentially immune from the insidious stressors that can make professional life miserable for other judges and, in some cases, cause burnout. A good reputation helps you avoid trouble and, if trouble comes, it helps you deal with it.

I consider it essential to acknowledge the presence of other people, to stop talking, and to listen to what they have to say. You must make yourself understood by not talking above or below them.

Isn't it insulting when another person does not acknowledge your presence and neither looks at you, speaks to you, nor includes you in a conversation with others? Isn't it insulting when another person uses language that you do not understand or uses a condescending tone? I have seen attorneys alienate people by speaking very slowly and using simple monosyllabic words as if they were talking to a child or, on the other hand, by using highly technical terms not understood by a lay person.

The Golden Rule of "Do unto others what you would have them do unto you" is the fundamental rule for establishing and keeping a good reputation.

Doing the Right Thing

In 2001, I presided over the trial of Dr. Dirk Greineder, who was charged with murdering his wife. The trial lasted six weeks and the jury found the doctor guilty. Tom Farmer, of the *Boston Herald*, was one of many reporters present at the trial, which was featured on Court TV. He attended the proceedings and interviewed witnesses, attorneys, and family members. After the trial, Mr. Farmer, as a media expert, was interviewed for several TV documentaries. He felt strongly that the evidence supported the jury's verdict and that the defendant was guilty. He has since co-authored the book *A Murder in Wellesley.*

Several years after the trial, developments in the law mandated public access to jury selection proceedings including during the individual examination of prospective jurors. Basically, an appellate court had ruled that members of the public, including the press, must be given a chance to be present for all examinations. The defendant in my case then filed a motion for a new trial, claiming that the press and others were not given that opportunity.

Mr. Farmer knew that the defendant was seeking a new trial on these grounds. His memory was that I had excluded the press from the examination of individual jurors and that the media did not complain. He knew full well that the defendant might get a new trial if members of the press had not been permitted in the room. Disclosing this could be a basis for a new trial for a person whom he felt was guilty beyond doubt. He put his personal feelings aside and did the right thing by writing a letter to me about his memory of the events.

On January 10, 2010, almost ten years after the trial, Mr. Farmer and about a dozen other people testified at a hearing before me. At the hearing, some people remembered that the courtroom was empty while others remembered that the courtroom was so crowded that it was almost impossible to find a seat.

I ultimately disagreed with some of Mr. Farmer's recollections and concluded that my order barred only media with cameras and video from the jury selection proceedings to protect juror privacy. This practice is still considered appropriate.

Mr. Farmer came forward under difficult circumstances and made an extremely positive and lasting impression on me. Doing the right thing is not always easy, but it's always right.

The Mystery of the Missing Pancake

We went to Hawaii recently with Bill and Margaret Mathisson. We spent a few nights on the Big Island of Hawaii with my old friend Addie Bowman and his wife, Jo, who live in a small house high in the mountains. It is in a remote location "off the grid" so that all of their electricity, heat, and hot water come from a number of solar panels on the roof and in the yard. They keep three dogs for security and to scare off wild animals. There is not much room in the house so Grandma and I slept on a mattress near the kitchen. After a couple of days, the Bowmans went to Oahu, the main island, and we spent a couple of nights in the house without them.

When we went to bed our last night there, we left a large leftover pancake on a plate on the kitchen counter, not far from where we were sleeping. In the morning the pancake had disappeared. Bill accused me of eating it and I accused him. It was a real mystery that perplexed all of us for many months. Finally, I had a chance to ask Addie about it.

He said that upon their return to their house, they discovered that a large rat had come in through a partially opened sliding door and was living in the bottom of the stove and had probably eaten the pancake. The rat ran out the way it got in and the dogs killed it.

Kind of creepy for a guy who has a phobia about rodents.

Biting the Lawyer's Hand

Recently, I was presiding over a drug session of the Superior Court in Middlesex County. A case was called by the clerk and the lawyer came forward with his client. The lawyer told me that he wanted to make a disclosure for the record and I responded that he could. He then told me that his client had been arrested for breaking and entering into a home two weeks earlier.

Knowing that some people get into trouble while their cases are pending, I thanked him. The lawyer immediately stated that I didn't understand, that his client had been arrested for breaking into the lawyer's house and stealing the lawyer's property.

At first it sounded like a very humorous story. It turned out to be quite sad. The lawyer was a distant relative of the defendant and he agreed to represent him for free. After the housebreak, the family asked him not to press charges and to continue representing the client. I had to spend significant time questioning the lawyer about his ability to represent someone who had broken into his house. I also questioned the defendant as to whether he really wanted to be represented by someone who must have been pretty mad at him. Both the lawyer and the client convinced me that the lawyer should continue representing the man.

The lawyer was faced with the dilemma of continuing to help a family member who had betrayed the lawyer's trust. The client told me that he felt that the lawyer could and would continue to do a good job. The lawyer said that he could forgive and forget about the incident. But all this would go out the window if the client lost the legal case and then complained that his lawyer was biased and didn't try hard enough.

Until Death Do Us Part Auto Warranty

I always buy my new cars from Dan Quirk, owner of Quirk Motors. I know him well and trust him. His lawyer is my good friend Phil Nyman, whom you may remember from *Bench Notes*. Phil and I often joke with one another. Whenever I have even a minor problem with a Quirk car, I always threaten Mr. Nyman that I will sue his client for consumer fraud even if the issue is a burned-out light bulb. My Quirk Nissan Maxima lasted for over 250,000 miles. I told Phil that I had a 350,000-mile warranty.

Recently, I purchased a black Nissan Sentra from Dan Quirk. I have an eight-year warranty and I told Phil Nyman that I wasn't sure whether his client had promised me the "Until Hell Freezes Over" or the "Until Death Do Us Part" bumper-to-bumper warranty. Phil responded that it was the "Until Death Do Us Part" warranty because they can arrange for that if need be. With really good friends, you can even joke about death. You cannot do so with others.

Savoir Vivre

When the Attorney's Oath is administered to new lawyers at Boston's historic Faneuil Hall, the Chief Justice often glibly advises the lawyers to be nice to judges because a judge can hurt them and to be extra nice to court clerks because a clerk can kill them. Attorney Lenny Kesten has a sign on his office door that reads, "A good lawyer knows the judge, a great lawyer knows the clerk." In court, the clerk manages the list and an offensive lawyer might find himself waiting the better part of the day for his case to be called. More importantly, an experienced clerk can give an attorney invaluable advice when proceeding before a particular judge.

These lessons also apply to life outside of the court. People often make the mistake of going to the top person whenever they want something. If I need something from my doctor, I often go through the nurse practitioner. She can either do what has to be done or get the doctor to do it without delay. I have seen customers in stores and at airline counters demand to see the person in charge under circumstances when the clerk or agent could solve the problem. This conduct often alienates the subordinate and places the supervisor in the position of supporting the subordinate to the detriment of the customer.

Recently, an attorney approached me during a court session seeking permission to rearrange all of the tables and chairs because the case involved several attorneys and their clients. I could see that the attorney had sidestepped the clerk and the court officers, who appeared miffed. I told the attorney to work it out with the staff. He should have known better. These are things that my French friend, the late Felix Faure, would say are part of *"savoir vivre,"* that is, developing the instinct of knowing how to live and what to do and what not to do.

Senior Running

I complained to a judge friend last June that I had just run in the Covered Bridges Half Marathon in Woodstock, Vermont, at a snail's pace and finished nearly last. My colleague congratulated me on the accomplishment and asked me if I knew what the last person in a medical school class is called. He answered his own question by replying, "Doctor." I then thought that the last person in an officer training class is not only called "Sir" or "Ma'am," but he or she is saluted as well. Reflecting on that, I did not hesitate to wear a T-shirt with the logo "13.1" that was a gift from Bob Lebowitz. Perhaps, I will even put a 13.1 sticker on my car.

Most of us are mediocre at some things, even things we enjoy. I have been, and always will be, mediocre at athletics and at music. I have played racquet sports since my teen years and as an adult have completed six marathons, several half marathons, and many 10K races.

Each November, I run with your parents in the 10-kilometer portion of the Marine Corps Marathon in Washington, D.C., and Virginia where there are several thousand entrants. Almost from the start of the race, I can see a line of thousands of people running in front of me. This year, the route had us running on an overpass at the 4-mile mark and beneath the overpass was the 3-mile mark. At 4 miles, I could look down and see hundreds of people who were at least one mile behind me. Of course, there were still thousands ahead of me, but, at that moment, it all came together as a lesson in life. Make the best of what you can do.

The Mouse That Roared[4]

My last civil jury trial involved a suit brought by a shoe store employee against the supermarket "anchor" store that owned the shopping center. The plaintiff was restocking shelves in the shoe store. She climbed a ladder and was placing boxes on the top shelf when a mouse leaped from the top shelf, ran down her extended arm, and then disappeared at floor level. She fell off the ladder screaming and suffered a back injury. She could not sue her employer because of the workers' compensation law. Instead, she sued the store's supermarket owner/landlord. The theory was that the mouse was in the store because of negligent maintenance of the grounds.

The plaintiff had a difficult case as the jury learned that all mice look the same and obviously, even if the offender was caught, good luck at interviewing it. A pond and marshland were nearby and we learned how many thousands of mice per square mile resided in such an area. A maintenance expert opined that the mouse could well have come from a delivery truck with boxes of shoes from open warehouses. We also learned about various preventive measures including closed Dumpsters, frequent trash removal, and sweeping of parking lots as well as the placing of bait and traps.

The supermarket owner of the shopping center was disappointed that I did not dismiss the case because of lack of evidence as to the origin of the offending mouse. I allowed the case to go to the jury and it rather quickly found against the plaintiff.

I do not like rodents and I thought that many jurors felt likewise and would not want to sit on the case. Of the 60 prospective jurors, not one indicated any uneasiness because of the subject matter of the case.

During the trial, I remembered my experience in the Grand Canyon when Grandma and I were staying in a dormitory shelter at the bottom of the canyon. I was asleep in a bunk bed when a mouse jumped on me and ran down my back. I didn't panic. Maybe it's because I have always felt that country mice are cleaner than city mice.

---

[4] *The Mouse that Roared* is the title of the 1959 classic movie comedy with Peter Sellers. It is about a tiny fictional country called the Duchy of Grand Fenwick that successfully invades the United States.

Poetry in Motion

I just passed my 75th birthday and realized that three of my four grandparents made it only this far. I attribute what mental acuity and physical abilities I have to decades of unrelenting mental and physical exercise.

My maternal grandfather, S. D. Aaronson, introduced me to poetry at age five. He bribed me with coins to learn a poem and keep it in memory for several months. I learned, and have kept in memory to the present, "Daffodils," "Flanders Fields," "Trees," "Invictus," and "Stopping by Woods on a Snowy Evening" as well as others. I read poetry during my early adult years but began in earnest to memorize poetry to stretch my mind when I turned 40 years old. Since then, I have always tried to keep at least 30 poems in memory including 10 Robert Frost poems, 10 Shakespearean sonnets, and 10 other poems or works. This being the 150th anniversary of the Gettysburg Address, I have memorized it. My quiet time for memorization is in the car while commuting. I have started you, my grandchildren, on Robert Frost poetry and I hope it will help illumine your lives for all time like it has mine.

I started running fairly regularly when I was chairman of the Parole Board at age 33. I ran with a fellow board member in South Boston along the ocean. Then Grandma and I ran together several times each week and your dad sometimes ran with us too. I ran three Boston Marathons, one time with Grandma and our dog, Betsy. I ran the New York City Marathon three times and the Montreal Marathon once.

Over the past 25 years I have been deeply indebted to my close friend Bob Lebowitz, who makes sure that I run at least four days per week. He is a retired physician and a serious athlete who will not allow me to slacken off. When I claim (or feign) illness, he almost always encourages me to run through it. He sometimes relents when I have a fever or the temperature outside is so low that frostbite is an issue.

My birthday is in late December and his is in late January. For the past 32 years we have taken off from work on the mornings of our birthdays and run together one minute for every year of age. The person whose birthday it is not then treats at breakfast. We have had some very cold and slippery birthday runs and some great breakfasts.

So, as I continue memorizing poetry and running in my 76th year, I have S. D. Aaronson (born 1882) and Bob Lebowitz (born 1940) to thank for these mind and body exercises.

S. D. Aaronson   Bob Lebowitz

The Hole Truth

I had to laugh when watching a report of some of the building construction for the 2014 Winter Olympic Games in Sochi. Some bathrooms contained two toilets with no wall separating them. We, of course, are accustomed to either private bathrooms with one toilet, or bathrooms with toilets located within individual stalls.

When I was growing up in New Haven, Connecticut, we lived close to a lumberyard that had a two-seater outhouse, a board with two holes about two feet apart. We kids shared the outhouse and there was never a thought of privacy.

Now, our farmhouse in Vermont has two full bathrooms with one toilet each. Grandma and I remember the days when there were no bathrooms at the farm. Instead, an outhouse with a board seat with two holes to accommodate two persons at one time was attached to the house. I don't ever remember sharing the board with anyone, but it did seem primitive at the time. A friend from Brooklyn visited for a few days and he suffered because he could not bring himself to use the facilities.

In 2001, I flew from Boston to Moscow and then from Moscow to Tomsk, Siberia. Grandma accompanied me on this legal/cultural exchange. We boarded the flight to Tomsk at about midnight and flew in a propeller-driven Russian airplane of World War II vintage. In the middle of the night I went to use the restroom and found no toilet, only a hole in the floor. I decided that I could wait, no matter what.

At the federal courthouse in Tomsk there were flush toilets with individual stalls in the basement. However, there was no toilet paper, only three-inch-wide strips of newspaper and a stack of newspapers on a common table. The protocol was to use the newspaper strips and afterward tear strips for the next person. Your dad says Russians are used to this because severe shortages became part of the culture during Soviet times.

The subject matter may be humorous, but what I take from it is that when it comes to personal hygiene, we are only comfortable with what we know.

A Marathon of Civility

In *Bench Notes,* I recalled how civil everyone was following the tragic terrorist attack on September 11, 2001. I made the same observations after the terrorist bombing at the Boston Marathon on April 22, 2013.

I perform mediation and arbitration work at the Brody, Hardoon, Perkins, and Kesten law firm, which is located on the 12th floor of an office building across the street from the Boston Public Library at Copley Square and within feet of the painted yellow finish line of the Boston Marathon. The first explosion occurred nearly in front of our building, maiming and killing several innocent spectators. The building was closed for ten days while police examined the crime scene and the contractors repaired damage to the building itself.

I take the subway train from Newton to Copley Square when I work in Boston. For at least one month after the Marathon, the subway cars were quiet, no one pushed or shoved at rush hour, and younger people seemed more inclined to offer their seats to others, including seniors.

The sidewalk outside of Marathon Sports (which is next to our office) is where the bomb actually exploded, causing the terrible injuries. For weeks, people gathered at that location to pay their respects to those injured or killed there. People also left bouquets of flowers on the ruptured sidewalk. Early one evening when I was returning to the office, I saw a man pick up a bouquet of flowers and start to walk away with them. Without thinking, I approached him and said, "Put those back." He did, and walked away. He was twice my size and half my age. Perhaps that was not smart of me, but I reacted as I believe most people would have at the time.

It's too bad that it takes a horrible event to remind us that we are all part of a community.

Boston Marathon Finish Line

Boston Marathon Memorial Exhibit
Boston Public Library, April 2014

Feeling Decisions

Judge Arthur Sherman was my mentor when I was appointed to the District Court thirty-eight years ago. He was ten years my senior. He died this year and I attended his funeral. Judge Sherman knew the law, wrote well, showed compassion, and promoted innovations. He had previously had a successful civil legal practice. When appointed to the bench, I had much experience with the criminal law, but little experience with the civil.

During my first month on the bench I tried a very complicated nonjury civil case. I had to decide the merits of the case and explain my reasoning in a memorandum of decision. I called Judge Sherman for help. I sat at his kitchen table and told him all about the case. After listening very attentively, he said that he was not going to make the decision for me. He instructed me to go home and write out all the facts of the case in longhand and when I was finished, I would know how the matter should be resolved. I only half-believed him, but went home and did it. He was absolutely right. I have applied that lesson time and time again, although my poor handwriting has pushed me towards word processing.

At a Superior Court Education Conference in the 1990s, our dinner speaker was author Doris Kearns Goodwin. She had just written "No Ordinary Time," which detailed the life of Eleanor Roosevelt. I sat next to our speaker at the dinner table before her presentation. I asked her whether she typed, dictated, or handwrote her books. She responded that she had to feel what she was composing and therefore wrote out by hand every word of every book. In a similar manner, Judge Sherman taught me how to feel my decision making.

The Book Cover

My case involved a fight with fists and a knife where the defendant stabbed and killed a member of a rival gang. He was charged with first-degree murder and the jury found him guilty of second-degree murder. After the jury was discharged and the courtroom was empty, a court officer and the defendant's attorney were standing next to the open door to the jury deliberation room where they saw a book on the window ledge that was left behind by a juror. The title of the book read "GUILTY" in large boldface letters.[5] The defendant's attorney immediately sought a new trial on grounds that the jury had been exposed to extraneous harmful evidence. On learning of these events, I went to my local library, borrowed a copy of the book, and spent the weekend reading it.

I found that the book's premise was that "liberals use any means to take unfair advantage of conservatives." Although the contents were political and didn't deal with cases such as the one before the court, the book's cover raised a legitimate inquiry. The cover appeared so provocative, that regardless of the book's content, the juror should not have brought it to read in the jury room during "down time." I later spent several hours in the courtroom listening to both attorneys argue why the verdict should stand or not stand. I ultimately decided that the book's cover, which included innocuous smaller print, would not encourage jurors to be unfair in their decision making. I found that the juror who had brought the book to court was only exposed to liberal/conservative political commentary that was irrelevant to the case.

"You can't tell a book by its cover" is an expression known to everyone. The question in my case was whether reading the cover alone could reasonably render a person unfair. My answer was that the defendant's attorney hadn't proven that the cover could have affected the verdict and the Appeals Court agreed. This experience has made me more sensitive to the book covers I see displayed in retail stores.

---

[5] In smaller print, the title included "Liberal 'Victims' and their Assault on America."

Much Ado About Nothing

There was a man who was in his eighties who fancied himself a handyman and tried to diagnose a homeowner problem for his single-parent daughter. He wasn't carrying a flashlight and carelessly lit a match in her basement to get a better view of the insulation between the inside and outside walls. The insulation caught fire and burned rapidly all the way up to the roof. The daughter's homeowner's insurance paid her for the property damage to her house. The insurance company then brought a subrogation lawsuit in the daughter's name against her elderly father, who had very limited assets.

A month before the scheduled trial date, the case came before me for resolution of pre-trial motions. I knew that the lawyer for the insurance company didn't have his heart in the case and I told him so. He said that the company insisted on pursuing it. I told him to tell the company that the pre-trial motions were so complicated that it might take me until retirement to resolve them. At the time, I was twenty years from retirement. He smiled and the case somehow disappeared.

It's disappointing when people or institutions either sue or defend a suit where their position has little or no merit. Even if there is technically some merit, there are instances like the one just described where common sense, ethics, or basic civility should discourage the use of the legal process.

Small Talk

The New England Journal of Medicine recently featured an article on "The Virtues of Irrelevance," which should be of equal interest to physicians and judges. The article teaches that seemingly irrelevant opening inquiries such as noting an article of clothing, a sports team interest, or the patient's home town promotes individuality, a sense of shared experiences, as well as the physician's attention to detail and openness. Initially speaking to a patient about things that are ostensibly irrelevant to the purpose of the medical visit enhances the quality of the visit and the confidence in the physician. The article concludes that this is more than a "nice touch" in that it supports a genuine connection between doctors and patients.

When a criminal defendant pleads guilty before a judge, a very formal colloquy is required. The judge and the defendant are often poles apart as to education, ethnicity, language, religion, upbringing, family values, and street savvy. A sensitive judge will start the colloquy with questions that demonstrate to the defendant that the judge is interested in him as more than a statistic in the disposition of a court case. Among other things, the judge should ask the defendant in detail about his immediate family. I ask the person to introduce me to family members who are in the courtroom and often I allow the mother or spouse to sit in the jury box close to the defendant during the guilty plea. During an initial inquiry, I have also learned amazing things about defendants, for example, an interest in poetry, musical talent, or a spelling proficiency.

Of course, the judge should show real sensitivity to the victim's interests too. When a victim is giving an oral victim impact statement to the judge in the courtroom, the judge should consider going that extra step and talk about seemingly irrelevant things to "break the ice" and convey a sense of worthiness. With a defendant or a victim, I have sometimes found commonality and shared things such as a migraine inheritance, interest in sports, and not smoking.

Shouldn't the "Virtues of Irrelevance" be a part of our daily communication with most people? There is absolutely nothing small about "small talk" when it demonstrates that we care about the other person as a person.

There's No Downside to Being Nice

When I became chairman of the state parole board, a politician reminded me of the old adage: "Be kind to people on the way up because you never know who you will meet on the way down."

A lawyer I know has always been nice to everyone. When he became very sick with a debilitating and protracted case of Lyme disease, the principal attorney at his law firm reduced his workload, purchased a couch, and insisted that he nap every afternoon.

I have been told that a couple of judges with reputations for being overbearing were very disappointed when denied the opportunity to return to service after reaching the mandatory retirement age of 70. A former prosecutor, who was very discourteous to defense lawyers for many years, has not succeeded in the private practice of law because not many lawyers will refer business to him.

Grandma reminds me that Shakespeare wrote about this almost four hundred years ago in *Julius Caesar*: "He then unto the ladder turns his back . . . scorning the base degrees by which he did ascend."[6]

---

[6] William Shakespeare, *Julius Caesar,* act II, scene 1 (Brutus justifying his own fear that Caesar will abuse power).

My Kingdom for a Card

Your Great-Granddad Arthur Wardwell was a proud veteran who served his country for 35 years. I am also a proud veteran, but with only 3.5 years of service. Art and I raised the American flag at the farm each morning we were there. We were very careful to not let it touch the ground. (In my day at the Naval Operations Base in Norfolk, Virginia, 100 pushups was the penalty for allowing the flag to touch the ground.)

Grandma and I, Bill and Margaret Mathisson, and Addie and Jo Bowman recently stayed at a military recreation facility open to servicemen and veterans on the Big Island of Hawaii. Addie, Bill, and I qualified as honorably discharged veterans. Only Addie carried proof and was able to vouch for us. Since then, I have tried in vain to obtain a veteran's identification card. I went to the Veterans' Administration in Vermont that I thought would be user friendly. I showed my discharge papers and my status was confirmed. However, the VA's rule is that ID cards go only to those receiving health care and financial benefits. The cards are manufactured in Tennessee. To the VA, the cost is prohibitive to issue cards to non-users of their services. I offered to pay for my own card, to no avail. I intend to contact one of my elected officials about convincing the Veterans' Administration to change its policy and give proper respect to all veterans.

Some veterans' groups have prevailed on their state motor vehicle departments to identify them as veterans on their drivers' licenses and/or license plates. Recently, I brought my discharge papers to the Registry of Motor Vehicles when I renewed my driver's license. I am proud that "VETERAN" is now printed on my license.

Great-Granddad raising the flag at the farm

Two Bad Peas in a Pod

On the same day, in two separate cases, two married fathers of young children pled guilty before me on charges of abusing their own children. The two abused children were about the same age, the abuse was very similar, and neither father had a criminal record. The only difference in the two cases was that one of the mothers wanted her husband to serve at least ten years in prison with no possibility of parole while the other mother wanted her husband to be placed on probation with a condition that he be involved with family therapy so he could eventually move back into the house. The two children were too young to express their opinions to me.

Do similar people who commit similar crimes deserve similar sentences or does the viewpoint of the victim or the victim's family make a substantial difference? In the first case, the prosecutor recommended five years in prison and the defense lawyer recommended one year. In the second case, the prosecutor recommended two years in prison while the defense lawyer recommended a period of probation with conditions of therapy.

The law allows the victim and/or a family member to give a victim impact statement in writing and/or in person in court to the judge. This should have some weight as to the sentence. However, it would be inappropriate for the victim to dictate the sentence.

When Governor Michael Dukakis ran for president against George H. W. Bush, he courageously maintained his position against the death penalty. During a nationally televised debate, Governor Dukakis was asked whether he would approve the death penalty for a criminal who raped and killed his wife. Dukakis responded by saying that the question was unfair because in our democratic system it's the judge and sometimes the jury who have the awesome task of sentencing. His measured response didn't play well in the theater of politics and may have helped account for his loss of support following the debate. But Dukakis got it right.

After considering each of the abuse cases, I sentenced both men to prison, but I gave them different sentences. In my mind, I justified that one crime was more serious than the other because it had a vastly different impact on the victim.

Thinking Outside the Box

My Trial Practice students at Boston College Law School hone their lawyering skills with mock or pretend cases that are based on my real-life court cases. One of the cases involved a young man charged with driving under the influence of alcohol. His defense was that he consumed only one beer and was not drunk. In class, on the evening for closing arguments, a student stood up to deliver his closing argument on behalf of the young man. As he spoke to the jury of law students, he opened up a can of beer and consumed it during his presentation. He closed by explaining that the jury could see that he was not drunk after one beer. It was clever, entertaining, informative and, of course, not appropriate for a real courtroom setting. I gave him an "A" because he thought "outside the box." He used his imagination to distinguish himself from all of the other students.

A screening panel responsible for hiring a person for an administrative position was to reduce the pool of twelve candidates to three. All of the candidates appeared very well qualified. Only one man stood out. He told the panel that proper administration requires juggling skills and, as uncoordinated as he might be, he had taught himself to juggle. He produced three balls and juggled them. He made the cut and was one of the three chosen for the final round.

It's important to distinguish yourself from others. I recall reading that you receive better service from a physician who remembers you. Grandma, who worked as a dental hygienist, says that the dental staff remembers the patient who brings the brownies. You really have to think "outside the box" to make a different kind of positive impression on those you encounter on a daily basis.

Is There a Doctor in the House?

I was presiding over a jury-waived criminal trial in the Cambridge Superior Court on December 18, 2002. At 10:15 A.M., the gentle, boyish-looking 51-year-old prosecutor put his hands to his head and collapsed five feet from the bench and me. Unbeknownst to me, he had suffered a fatal brain aneurism. I stood there, in my authoritative black robe, with no power to remedy the situation. Had I been a doctor I could not have saved him, but I still think about whether I might have missed some early sign and done something about it.

My mother used to brag to her friends that she had one son who was a doctor and one who was a judge. My parents were pharmacists and I suppose that I went into engineering instead of healthcare in a rebellious reaction to listening to them discuss pharmaceuticals with my brother Bob while he was a pre-med student at Yale and then a medical student at Tufts.

With a smile, Captain Jack Boyer designated me as the "medical officer" on the ship *Bowie* because of my close "family relationship" to medicine. I held a sick call for village residents when we docked at small landlocked Alaskan towns. After I graduated from law school, my brother suggested that I go to medical school and join him in practice. I declined, but have often wondered how that would have turned out.

My strength as a judge has been my judicial "bedside manner," which is probably akin to the bedside manner expected of doctors. After the tragic death in my courtroom, I heard that Harvard Medical School was considering admitting a couple of applicants over 50 years of age. Friends encouraged me, but it turned out they were not focused on people over 60.

I have taken several career paths over the years including engineer, commissioned officer, patent lawyer, public defender, parole agency head, judge, and mediator. I think it's important to seek variety and not to get stuck in unpleasant work or an unpleasant work environment.

Don't get yourselves in a rut. Consider jumping ship to a new path to avoid the limited choice in life described by Robert Frost in "The Road Not Taken."

"The Road Not Taken"

Two roads diverged in a yellow wood,
And sorry I could not travel both
And be one traveler, long I stood
And looked down one as far as I could
To where it bent in the undergrowth;

Then took the other, as just as fair,
And having perhaps the better claim,
Because it was grassy and wanted wear;
Though as for that, the passing there
Had worn them really about the same,

And both that morning equally lay
In leaves no step had trodden black.
Oh, I kept the first for another day!
Yet knowing how way leads on to way,
I doubted if I should ever come back.

I shall be telling this with a sigh
Somewhere ages and ages hence:
Two roads diverged in a wood, and I—
I took the one less traveled by,
And that has made all the difference.

Grandpa at the Robert Frost Interpretive Trail
in Ripton, Vermont

Skill, Strength, and Perseverance

One of our summer chores in Vermont is to cut, split, and stack wood for heating the house during the cool fall days and cold nights. I remember one time when Great-Granddad Art was in his nineties. He, your dad, and I used a chain saw to cut up a large maple tree that was lying across the road from the farmhouse. We used a cart to bring the log pieces to an area just outside the barn in order to split them with an axe. Some of the hard maple measured more than one foot in diameter and, to me, splitting them was going to be quite a chore.

Art approached the first piece and swung the axe once and it split immediately. Art had been splitting wood since he was a boy on that farm and he learned to "read" wood. That is, he could examine the grain and know exactly where and how to strike it with the axe for easy splitting. He did not look like he was even exerting himself as he easily split the log into four pieces. Great-Granddad then handed the axe to your dad, who was in his mid-thirties.

Your dad does not have decades of experience splitting wood and he could not read wood like Art could. However, he is very strong from years of exercise. He swung the axe with all of his might and the wood split on either the first or second blow. I was very impressed with his accomplishment, but we knew that it paled in comparison to Art's. He then handed the axe to me.

As a "flatlander," I never developed the Vermonter's ability to read wood and, in my mid-sixties, I did not have the strength of one thirty years my junior. I read the wood as best as I could and swung the axe as hard as I could. It merely embedded itself in the log and I had to pry it out for the next swing. I persevered and must have hit that damn piece ten times before it split. I think it was your dad who complimented me on the making of toothpicks for the dining room.

Life requires a honing of all three attributes. For example, a skillful mediator or jurist can read the grain of the human condition at work in each particular case. A strong mediator or jurist works hard to overcome or deflect contentiousness and base emotions. A mediator or jurist perseveres by exercising patience in chipping away at differences and finding commonality among the adversaries.

Art, Paul, and Steven   Steven Chernoff

<u>Truth or Consequences</u>[7]

Some attribute this saying to Mark Twain: "A lie can get half-way around the world before the truth can get its boots on." Somewhere along the way, the truth usually catches up.

Harmless lies or "fibs" are a part of everyday living, such as, "I really like your hairdo" or "If he calls, tell him I'm not at home." These, we forgive and forget. However, those who tell harmful lies with the intention of hurting others will likely suffer very bad consequences when the lies catch up with them

Recently, the truth caught up to the lies and deceptions of an insurance company and its lawyers in an accident case where a pedestrian was seriously injured after he was hit by a bus. A report by the bus driver's insurance company's investigator and his recorded interview of a key witness were concealed and a new version of the events was planted with the witness through inappropriate coaching by the lawyers.

These improprieties were exposed by the injured man's attorneys, Lenny Kesten and Rick Brody.[8] The consequences to the offending insurance company will involve the payment of a very large sum of money and the consequences to the wrongdoing lawyers may well be severe discipline.

Aside from hurting an innocent person, a liar also violates the trust of that person and others. There is really no downside to telling the truth, even where you did something wrong and you are embarrassed by it. Most often people will try their best to understand, forgive you, and perhaps even reward you for having the courage to tell the truth.

---

[7] An NBC radio show hosted by Ralph Edwards that premiered in 1940. Later, NBC and CBS broadcasted it on television until 1988. In the show, a contestant's failure to answer a trivia question resulted in an embarrassing stunt.

[8] I am a part-time mediator and arbitrator at the Boston law firm of Brody, Hardoon, Perkins, and Kesten.

Proofreading and Hindsight Bias

I learned some important lessons in life from the writing of the first *Bench Notes* book. First, the author should never rely on himself for proofreading. There is a human phenomenon that makes people very forgiving of their own work and blind to their mistakes. One week before printing, I was waiting for a flight at Logan Airport with my friend Jim Mangraviti, a principal of SEAK, Inc. We were en route to train expert witnesses in Las Vegas. I had proofread the back cover of my book many times. Jim, who was seated next to me, looked over and pointed out two typos. Fortunately, there was time to correct them. Jim is a prolific author and he advised me that proofreading and editing of one's work must be done by a total stranger to the work.

After my book was printed and two hundred copies were in circulation, I was very confident that the book was in perfect typographical form. I was shocked to learn from an attorney friend that there was an error on a particular page. I believe it read "piece" rather than "peace" and it wasn't caught by a spell or grammar check computer function. I had read that page at least a dozen times. When I turned to the page, I didn't have to read it because the error jumped off the page at me. I learned from my radiologist friend, Dr. Michelle Silvera, that I had experienced another human phenomenon, that of "hindsight bias." Radiologists know it well when looking for hard-to-find things on X-rays. If you are looking for something specific or have reason to know something is there you will easily find it. But if you are engaged in a specific search for something else such as a fracture or don't have reason to know something else is there such as a tumor, you may miss it despite being observant and careful. Once you know or suspect something is there, it becomes obvious to you, but not to others.

These lessons play out in everyday living. We tend not to be self-critical and we should understand and account for the fact that others may see us in a different light. As to hindsight bias, remember that others may not see things that are obvious to us when we know what to look for. For example, if someone tells you that I may have a spot on my tie, if it's there, you will see it from a distance while others may never notice it. We should be aware of "hindsight bias" and not judge others too harshly.

Diversity

Years ago, four juveniles pled guilty before me to pulling a fire alarm and running away. These matters are treated seriously because of the risk of harm to people from a responding emergency vehicle and because of the financial expense to the community. While I maintained a stern demeanor in the courtroom, I was nevertheless charmed and heartened by the composition of the group of miscreants that included a Jewish boy, an Italian boy, an African-American boy, and an Asian boy. I'm used to cases with warring street gangs with memberships based on race or ethnicity. I tried to picture my diverse group reaching adulthood as friends and doing productive things together.

The student population in my grammar school and junior high school in New Haven, Connecticut, was almost entirely Italian, Irish, African-American, and Jewish. I may have met my first Protestant in high school. I didn't realize they were in the majority until I reached college. Grandma jokingly says that I married the first Protestant girl I met.

Diversity can be the catalyst for strong lifetime bonds between people. Among my friends are Joe Annunziata, whom I have known since the second grade, Bill Mathisson, my West Coast roommate on the ship *Pathfinder* and ship *Bowie*, Judge John Cratsley with his Quaker upbringing, Clerk/Magistrate Mike Brennan, whom I call my Irish brother, and Supreme Judicial Court Judge Geraldine Hines, an African-American colleague. Had we been fourteen-year-olds living in the same town, I think we would have been friends, though it's unlikely the six of us would have pulled a fire alarm.

Ode to Judges and the Rest of Us

As a senior judge, I sometimes speak at judicial education conferences about judicial endurance and averting burnout. At such meetings, we have had occasion to discuss great poetry.

Recently, one judge found special meaning in a passage from "Ode on a Grecian Urn." He saw the judge's role as almost exclusively that of a truth finder in an environment where few people tell the whole truth. I gather that, in his view, the beauty of judging was determining the truth. Of course, he was making reference to the immortal lines of John Keats:

> *When old age shall this generation waste,*
> *Thou shalt remain, in midst of other woe*
> *Than ours, a friend to man, to whom thou say'st,*
> *"Beauty is truth, truth beauty,"—that is all*
> *Ye know on earth, and all ye need to know.*

I thought the judge was wrong, at least as to his priorities. Truth, if you can find it, is cold and stark while beauty is mostly skin deep. Determining the true facts is only the first step as real judging involves what we then do about it. Judging is clearly much more than calling balls and strikes. It was so heartening to hear the other judges substitute for truth and beauty, "patience," "understanding," "kindness," "compassion," "forgiveness," "understanding human frailty," "compromise," and "reconciliation." I suspect that Keats was prodding us to look beyond superficially appealing concepts and be more than umpires.

Connectivity

One of life's greatest lessons is that we need not feel abandoned and all alone. I have, without quoting Richard Lovelace, essentially told people I was sentencing and their family members that "Stone walls do not a prison make."[9] Prisoners must strive to stay connected with those who care, even when they are far away.

This lesson is taught in a more subtle fashion by Robert Frost in "The Tuft of Flowers." His opening lines are the most beautiful of any poem I know.

> *I went to turn the grass once after one*
> *Who mowed it in the dew before the sun.*

After dawn, the narrator comes to turn over the grass that was cut with a scythe before dawn by a man who had already left. The narrator, as he starts his task, feels totally alone and abandoned until he sees that the cutter had left intact an area by a brook for birds, butterflies, and other living things. Sharing the cutter's purpose, the narrator then feels a brotherly kinship and concludes with these memorable lines:

> *"Men work together," I told him from the heart,*
> *"Whether they work together or apart."*

From my perch, Frost could be talking to judges who live monastic lives imposed by the rules of judicial conduct. Feeling isolated when seated alone on the bench or when immersed in a public maelstrom, a judge can and must stay connected to others who can both listen and be guiding stars.

---

[9] "To Althea, from Prison" (Richard Lovelace)

Stone walls do not a prison make,
Nor iron bars a cage:
Minds innocent and quiet take
That for a hermitage;
If I have freedom in my love,
And in my soul am free,
Angels alone that soar above
Enjoy such liberty.

"Take Something Like a Star" (Robert Frost)

So when at times the mob is swayed
To carry praise or blame too far,
We may take something like a star
To stay our minds on and be staid.

Baseball and a "Mensch" at Fenway Park

July 20, 2014, was a warm, dry sunny day, perfect for baseball. For you, Rayan, at age 9, and for you, Dhillon, at age 7, it was your long-awaited first taste of Fenway Park. The Red Sox were playing the Royals. You and your dad placed your tickets in the machine at the gate and were admitted. My ticket was rejected. On inspection, it was for July 30th, not the 20th. The person from whom I received the tickets made a mistake and now I did not have a ticket for this game. The gray-haired security person at the gate looked at the two of you wearing your Red Sox caps, and then looked at me carrying your baseball gloves, and he whispered, "Go on in." The man was a real *mensch*, that is, a real human being. Baseball brings that out in people.

My father, William Chernoff, was an avid Brooklyn Dodgers' fan and he instilled a love of baseball in my brother Bob and me. In his final years, my father's personality soured because of a disabling stroke. It has been difficult for me to remember him before his illness, with one exception, our love of baseball. I can never forget our annual pilgrimages to see our Brooklyn Dodgers. When I was 10 years old, we shared the delight of seeing Jackie Robinson steal home. We were in tears when the Giants' Bobby Thompson ended our 1951 baseball season with a legendary home run known as the "shot heard 'round the world." I thank baseball for uniting us and for the memories.

Your dad and I played catch outside our Newton home every nice day for about ten years, that is, until he was in high school and thought it didn't look "cool." I found a back-up player in Ed Ginsburg. A couple of years later, your dad went off to Colby College and on his first visit home, he insisted on playing catch even though it was football season and pretty cold. It's a thrill to throw a baseball with the two of you and your dad outside our house in the same location where we used to play catch. I thank baseball for this connection between our three generations.

Baseball talk can encourage trust and friendship. It has helped Dr. Bob Lebowitz communicate with young patients and their parents at Children's Hospital and it has also helped me in speaking with crime victims in my office. Baseball talk has not worked for me in the courtroom. I remember a trial with Attorney Jay Lynch where I told the jury with a smile that we would be finishing early because I had a "religious commitment" at Fenway Park for Opening Day. I then put a Red Sox cap on my head. Not one juror even smiled.

Saving St. Nick

A judge serves on "Emergency Response" for one week each year, taking after-hours calls and making on-the-spot judgments on such matters as search warrants, restraining orders for domestic violence, mental health commitments, and bail for arrested persons. I usually volunteered to serve the week of Christmas in place of a judge who was observing Christmas.

One Christmas Eve, I was called to a quaint New England town on the North Shore, about an hour's drive from my Newton home. The local police had told me that it was an absolute emergency requiring my immediate presence at the police station. A woman had been arrested for violating a restraining order. She had joint custody of her children but was barred by a court order from contact with her ex-husband and his home. This is a small town and a police officer, who happened to be driving by the husband's house, saw the woman's car outside and suspected she was violating the restraining order. He arrested her.

When I arrived at the police station to conduct a bail hearing, a police officer and a few citizens from the community were there to tell me that the woman in the jail cell was the local church's choir director and she was scheduled to lead the choir for the Christmas Eve service at the church within the hour. I ordered her release and then came home and lit my Hanukkah candles.

The Cat's Meow

I looked in the mirror in my chambers and saw a gray-haired robed person who, after combing his hair, was about to be addressed as "Your Honor" by countless others in the courtroom. I was the "cat's meow" until I quickly brought myself down to earth by recalling Robert Frost's narrator in "For Once, Then, Something" who often knelt at well curbs and, peering into the well, saw a "shining surface picture of himself, godlike, looking out of a wreath of fern and cloud puffs." For an instant, that was I. Thank you, Robert Frost, for the reminder.

I have often been asked about my career path to the judiciary. I used to talk about taking Frost's "The Road Not Taken" because there are 43,000 lawyers in my state and about 410 judges. In later years I have been more honest with myself and talk about Frost's "The Fear of God," which should be required reading for all public officials.

> *If you should rise from Nowhere up to Somewhere,*
> *From being No one up to being Someone,*
> *Be sure to keep repeating to yourself*
> *You owe it to an arbitrary god*
> *Whose mercy to you rather than to others*
> *Won't bear too critical examination.*

Remember, nobody is perfect and, in fact, every one of us is a mixed bag. Anyone who tells you differently is probably looking for something from you.

Strict Seniority

Decisions that are made solely on the basis of seniority, to the exclusion of merit, are almost always unfair, unjust, and potentially hurtful.

By tradition, the sitting justices of the Massachusetts Superior Court line up by seniority when entering and being seated at funeral services for deceased judges. According to the tradition, retired judges enter randomly after the others. Over my thirty-year tenure on the Superior Court, I have not been able to persuade the powers that be that the tradition serves no purpose and can appear pompous to the public. At a recent public memorial service, I stood with the group of retired judges relegated to the back of the pack. Even though most of us had given the majority of our professional lives to the court we were treated as stragglers. Most of us tried to handle it with humor.

My strong distaste for strict seniority goes back more than fifty years. After graduation from college, I reported to the Naval Operations Base (NOB) in Norfolk, Virginia, for the three-month Officer Training Program on the Ship *Explorer*. I was the first recruit of seven to arrive at the navy base. Seniority was established by the order of reporting but someone got it backward. I thought it was no big deal being outranked by the others, as it affected only relatively minor matters like having a stateroom next to the loud propeller, sitting at the far end of the wardroom table, and receiving somewhat less responsible assignments. However, imagine learning years later that the strict seniority system governed our order of promotion to lieutenant (junior grade) and then to full lieutenant. I can understand how a mistake can mix up the order of seniority, but I cannot countenance the use of strict seniority to allow leaders to take the easy way out when making important decisions.

Seniority should be only one factor when considering promotions. Who better for advancement than someone who has demonstrated merit over the long run? For public judicial ceremonies, I would opt for random entrances for all judges who, after all, are a family of professional siblings.

Explorer Officer Training Class, July 1961
Ensign Paul A. Chernoff by seniority on right

When the Shoe's on the Other Foot

Should the criminal "go free because the constable has blundered" is a famous quote from the renowned jurist Benjamin Cardozo that has touched off almost a century of debate.[10] All trial judges have, on occasion, excluded evidence and dismissed criminal cases where law enforcement has illegally arrested, searched, or interrogated a person or where important legal procedures have not been followed. The purpose of this policy is to encourage government agents to act appropriately in that government should gain nothing when it acts inappropriately. A cynical public may see it as getting off on a technicality. I have often wondered how an offender feels when his case is dismissed on a so-called technicality. Is he relieved, does he think he has beaten the system and offend again, is it a wake-up call to shape up, or what?

      Last summer I received a traffic citation for driving too fast on a rural road while on vacation out of state. I paid the ticket by mail after checking off "no contest" on the form. Well, lo and behold, months later, I received the amount of my check back in the mail with a note explaining that the matter had been dismissed because the papers had not been filed on time in accordance with the law. I felt exceedingly lucky. Perhaps I should have felt that an injustice had resulted. Perhaps I should have wondered how many other motorists have also been let off because the constable blundered. I would like to think that the traffic stop itself was enough of a deterrent for me to watch my speed.

---

[10] *People v. Defore*, 150 N.E. 585, 587 (1926). Justice Cardozo was a judge on the New York Court of Appeals before being elevated to the United States Supreme Court.

A Lesson While Running on Wildcat Road

Grandma's farmhouse on Wildcat Road in Chittenden, Vermont, is the starting point for my early morning summer runs. I turn left and go up, really up, the dirt road for two to three miles before turning around and following the nameless brook that I call West Running Brook in honor of Robert Frost's poem of that name. Lately, on my return run, I seem to be following a heron that glides over the water while I trudge along the road. One morning, he almost waited for me while I slowed to exchange pleasantries with a neighbor.

I am reminded of Frost's poem "The Wood-Pile." The narrator finds himself deep in the forest approaching an abandoned woodpile while a little bird flies from tree to tree ahead of him. His haunting lines are,

> "... *like one who takes*
> *everything said as personal to himself*."

Some see this as a window on Frost himself. I don't know about that, but I do know people who seem to take everything personally. They are easily bothered, insulted, and made insecure by relatively mild actions of others. The decorum of a courtroom insulates judges from many of these things because, after all, few people gain from alienating a judge. However, judges become pretty well attuned to picking up on indirect communication and some are overly sensitive to what may or may not be criticism and what may or may not even relate to the judge. There is a wonderful French expression:

Si vous cherchez la bagarre	*If you look for trouble*
Vous trouverez la bagarre	*You will find trouble*

I was not stalking the heron and I know he was not waiting for me. I hope that he was not bothered by my actions. I remember years ago sitting in my office with my feet propped up on a lower desk drawer while awaiting a visit from a judge from Thailand. Fortunately, before the judge's arrival, someone advised me that elevating one's feet could be seen as an insult in his culture. Even an innocent remark to one from a foreign culture can be misconstrued and sour a relationship. When we feel threatened, insulted, or hurt by something said or done by another, we should try to stand in their shoes and judge their intentions before reacting.

Using Naughty Words

Most of the verbal communication in a courtroom is of a polite, respectful nature and often the speaker appears scholarly, sincere, and appropriately persuasive. However, the emotion of the moment occasionally penetrates the veneer of civility and we hear language that might make a sailor blush. I have heard, and have heard of, language that I would hesitate to repeat to anyone. I was going to recount some humorous events in the courtroom regarding the use of obscene language, but something inside me told me that it was not appropriate for this book, even though I have received advice to the contrary from many people.

In one case, a defendant and then the judge used a derogatory word that refers to a private part of a woman's body. I asked more than a dozen people whose judgment I trust about whether the word should appear in a vignette in this book. All the women but one said that I should definitely use it because the underlying story is interesting and humorous and everyone has heard the word before. About half of the men expressed reluctance because they felt it demeans women and was "over the top" as inappropriate language.

Last week was the acid test for me. I was giving a lecture to a group of senior citizens at Brandeis University on the subject of "professional endurance" and there was time at the end of my presentation to tell some funny R-rated or X-rated stories, with their permission. I had no problem using the "F word" and no problem talking about one of my cases where a man wanted the return of his expensive engagement ring after the wedding was called off. The engagement ring in this case was a clitoral ring. Then, when it came to my last story, I couldn't bring myself to tell it, even though I would be using words uttered by others.

As for you, there are not many occasions when you should stoop to use foul language. If the emotion of the moment causes you to express yourself with bad words, be very sure of your audience before uttering them. If someone utters off-color words to you or in your presence, try not to respond and don't give your approval for the other person's choice of words.

Operating Under the Influence

During my professional life, I have operated under the lasting influence of two luminaries: Judge William B. Bryant, the Chief Judge of the United States District Court for the District of Columbia, and Commissioner John O. Boone, the Commissioner of Correction for the Commonwealth of Massachusetts.

In June of 1970, I stood before the United States Supreme Court. Each justice nodded with full respect to the man who was moving my admission to the Court. Judge William B. Bryant was my mentor from the time I joined the Public Defender Service in 1967 to his death in 2005. He was the first African-American to be appointed to the position of Chief Judge of a federal district court. He was the wisest and most compassionate jurist I ever encountered. His chambers were a sanctuary for us public defenders who were sometimes unpopular elsewhere, being sullied by those we were appointed to represent. His wisdom and understanding of the human condition came from deep within. He could take a complicated or a contentious matter and bring it down to earth with one of his homespun analogies such as, "That's like going hunting and handing the bear the gun." I visited Judge Bryant in his chambers every year until his death. We were good friends as judges, but I always referred to him and addressed him as "Judge Bryant."

Also, in 1970, I filed a lawsuit against the superintendent of the prison in Lorton, Virginia, on behalf of inmates who were challenging prison conditions. Superintendent John O. Boone used the lawsuit as a device to obtain the resources to improve the challenged conditions. He absolutely won my heart and within months I started the "Lawyers for Lorton" bar association project where young lawyers visited the prison and helped inmates with civil legal matters facing them and their families. John Boone was recruited for the position of Commissioner of Correction in Massachusetts. He, in turn, recruited me to serve as the Chairman of the Parole Board. Commissioner Boone remained optimistic in the face of racist opposition and stiff resistance to his community corrections initiatives. He weathered "firestorms" on a daily basis, including prisoner riots and job actions by guards, as well as political and press criticism. I worked with him on almost a daily basis. He was the bravest and one of the most compassionate men I have ever known.

Judge William B. Bryant   Comm. John O. Boone

I'm Not King Solomon

When I was appointed to the bench, new judges were not offered introductory judicial education or training. I had little experience in juvenile matters, especially in gauging child neglect. Yet, within one month, I had the awesome responsibility of deciding whether the natural mother or an approved foster mother should have custody of an eighteen-month-old child. I thought to myself, how can a former public defender and parole board chairman make this Solomonic decision? It turned out that, after considering evidence from expert and lay witnesses and consulting with more senior judges, I could and did make the particular decision although judicial training would certainly have helped. This experience has made me a lifelong advocate of judicial education. Fortunately, now all new judges receive training that includes mentoring from experienced judges for their entire first year. Also, focused mentoring and continuing judicial education are available for all judges.

Our cases are so diverse that judicial education cannot cover everything. There are many times when a judge must decide issues in totally unfamiliar areas. For example, I had to declare the winner of a municipal election, to decide whether prison conditions met constitutional standards, and to rule whether a child should be given a life-saving blood transfusion over the objections of his Jehovah Witness parents.

I have since received formal training to be a judicial mentor and am called upon from time to time to assist a judge who is in need of help. Often the younger judges are very adept at using electronic devices and they feel that it is easier or better to seek answers on the Internet rather than to consult an experienced judge. I remember telling one of my mentees that he was not going to learn how to achieve more respect in the courtroom by surfing the Internet.

You can find an amazing amount of information from an electronic device, but often the information and advice that you really need must come from a person whom you really trust. Google can't teach you judgment.

My First Mediation

After my second retirement from the bench, I began work as a mediator and arbitrator of legal disputes. As a mediator, I work with the litigants and their attorneys and help them resolve their dispute by reaching a compromise solution. As an arbitrator, I consider evidence from each side and make the decision for them.

A property owner submitted a claim to his insurer for damage to his property. The insurer rejected the claim on grounds that the policy was void because the owner did not disclose certain risks at the time the policy was taken out. After the claim was rejected, the company continued to bill for premiums, which the owner paid. The property owner brought suit.

At the mediation hearing before me, the property owner and the insurer were at first miles apart. Both parties seemed angry. The insurance company suggested that the nondisclosure could be seen as fraudulent while the property owner suggested that billing and taking money for a "void" policy could be seen as an unfair trade practice. As we discussed the conduct of both parties, each side became less defensive, realized the significance of their own mistakes and, more importantly, understood that the other party's mistakes were unintentional. This process brought the parties closer and closer and the case settled that day.

Grandma, your dad, and I learned a wonderful French song during our six-week total immersion French program at Trois Pistoles, Quebec, when your dad was 12 years old. The song's title is "Pour un Instant" or, "For a Moment."[11] The recording by the group Harmonium is awesome. The second stanza mirrors my first mediation case.

Pour un instant j'ai retourné mon mirroir.	For an instant I turned my mirror around.
Ça ma permis enfin de mieux me voir.	That permitted me to better see myself.

---

[11] Written by band members Serge Fiori and Michael Normandeau.

An Old Dog Learns New Trick

As you know, a mediator helps the parties and their lawyers resolve their disputes through compromise and an arbitrator resolves their disputes by making the decisions for them. I am normally paid by the hour for this work.

One of my first cases involved fire damage to a farm building located more than fifty miles from my home. The weekend before the mediation, Grandma and I drove to the property out of a sense of curiosity. At the hearing, I informed the parties and their attorneys that I had visited the property on my own time at no cost to them. They were very moved by the fact that I gave up my time to help them. In other words, they were impressed that I showed that I cared about them. That lesson made a real impression on me.

Now, I often visit accident scenes, buildings, and other places on my own time before meeting with the parties to a dispute. For a recent arbitration I visited the roadway where a pedestrian was struck by a car at about the same time of day as the accident. At a mediation last week, the knowledge that I visited the scene of their gravel pit seemed to break the ice at a mediation of a family dispute. In a mediation with Chinese people, I brought apples as snacks because I had learned that the word "apple" in Mandarin Chinese also means "peace." People are impressed when they know that you care about them.

This year, Grandma and I took a boat trip from Washington State to Alaska. A court officer, knowing of my planned trip, brought me a brochure he had kept from his own trip there. It was such a thoughtful thing to do that it really cemented my relationship with him.

When you do something for someone that is neither expected nor required, the payback is often astonishing. Showing that you care is one of the best investments you can make.

My Retirement

The law required me to retire at age 70. Immediately, people congratulated me on my retirement. Although they meant well, I think they were merely engaging in a silly ritual. The truth is that retirement is a bitter pill for many judges who complain that the law says that they officially turn senile when they turn 70.

However, the law does permit the recall of a retired judge who can be selected by the Chief Justice to serve during a period of need. I retired December 20th, flew to Virginia with Grandma to visit you and your parents, and returned to serve on recall one week later at the behest of my chief justice, Barbara Rouse. Three and one-half years later, I retired again and started to work as a mediator and arbitrator at a Boston law firm. Six months later, the Chief Justice persuaded me and four other retired judges to return to service as special judicial magistrates to resolve court cases stemming from a scandal at a state drug laboratory. For two years now, I have worked part time as a special judicial magistrate and part time as a mediator/arbitrator at the law office. I also spend one day per week as a volunteer mediator for the Superior Court where at least one party cannot afford to pay a private mediator.

The work and people are interesting and, more important, I feel at home and appreciated at each courthouse and at the law office. This, coupled with the good health that Grandma and I share, has made our retirement years quite pleasant. Too many people become depressed soon after retirement. They age quickly and their health declines. Some of my colleagues couldn't wait to retire early and then quickly regretted it because they were bored, lonely, or needed additional income.

Of course "Poetry in Motion"—my nickname for running—has followed me into retirement as four or five mornings each week, at 6:30 A.M., I am greeted at the door by Dr. Lebowitz, who carefully explains to me before our run that cold, wind, and snow are character builders and that no self-respecting germ or virus would live in a body that is exposed to these elements. I fall for it every time.

My Usual Suspects

If there is an afterlife, I would like to spend it with a number of friends and family members from this life, but I would insist that I spend it with these five who have guided me through life on a daily basis.

Grandma Lynn Chernoff and I have been married for 50 years. She has supported me through both good and challenging times. She first translated Russian at the Library of Congress and then worked as a dental hygienist for 26 years. She is well read, plays the piano, and walks for exercise. She ran for many years and one April we ran the Boston Marathon together with our standard poodle, Betsy. Lynn has bonded with her ancestral farm in Chittenden, Vermont, and we are encouraging you three grandchildren to bond with your roots.

Judge John Cratsley and I met as legal aid lawyers in Washington, D.C., in the late 1960s. I followed John to Massachusetts and we had parallel careers as government agency heads, District Court judges, Superior Court judges, judicial magistrates, and mediators. John introduced me to the great outdoors starting with numerous canoe trips in the wilds of northern Maine. Later we organized our "Judicial Outward Bound" expeditions to the National Parks. A product of his Quaker upbringing, John has caused me to be less judgmental.

Dr. Bob Lebowitz is a retired physician. For over three decades we have been running together. I once computed that we have run a total number of miles equivalent to the distance around the earth at our latitude and, by now, perhaps at the equator. For decades we have been playing hooky on our respective birthdays, December 20th and January 26th. We run one minute for each year of age. Bob is an introspective person who is well read and who appreciates classical music and Shakespeare.

Judge Ed Ginsburg is my neighbor. We have walked together almost every night for the past forty years. No one else will join us as we are accused of having a 500-word vocabulary and are stuck on the subject of the Boston Red Sox. We teach together at Boston College Law School and elsewhere and are known as the "dynamic duo." After serving as a family court judge for 30 years he retired to two jobs, training legal service lawyers and running a program that matches volunteer senior lawyers with people who need lawyers in the family courts.

Steven Chernoff is my son, advisor, and best friend. We played catch every day for a decade during his formative years. I could beat him at racquetball, tennis, and running and now I can't get a point off of him. Last year he finished an hour ahead of me in a half marathon and this year he and Naina finished about 20 minutes ahead of me in the Marine Corps Marathon 10K race. Now he edits my writings and offers me solid advice on a full range of life's issues. With our depth of mutual love and respect, one could ask for no more.

In life, we are often defined by our experiences and by the people we really know.

ROGUES' GALLERY

Paul Chernoff

Lynn Chernoff

Thelma & Bill Chernoff

Steven Chernoff

Naina Chernoff

S. D. Aaronson

Rayan Chernoff

Dhillon Chernoff

Aliya Chernoff

Evelyn Wardwell

Art Wardwell

Bob Chernoff

Judy Chernoff

Norma Horwitch

Naomi Spector

Harvey Spector

Holly Cratsley   John Cratsley

Barbara Rouse   Geraldine Hines   Carol Ball

Bill Mathisson   Margaret Mathisson   Cathy Moritz

Ed Ginsburg

Julie Ginsburg

Bob Wadsworth

Helen Lebowitz

Bob Lebowitz

Phil Nyman

Rick Brody

Lenny Kesten

Vivian Kesten

Jim Mangraviti   Michael Brennan

Jay Lynch   Michelle Silvera